Nothing Else Matters

METALLICA

THIS IS A CARLTON BOOK

Text copyright © 2003 Chris Ingham
Design copyright © 2003 Carlton Publishing Group

Published by Thunder's Mouth Press
An Imprint of Avalon Publishing Group Incorporated
161 William St., 16th Floor
New York, NY 10038

Published in Great Britain by Carlton Books Limited,
20 Mortimer Street, London, W1T 3JW

Library of Congress Cataloging-in-Publication Data

ISBN 1-56025-536-6

EXECUTIVE EDITOR: Roland Hall
DESIGN: Lucy Coley/Barbara Zuñiga
PICTURE RESEARCH: Elena Goodinson
PRODUCTION: Lisa Moore

ACKNOWLEDGEMENTS/SOURCES
(1) *Metallica: In Their Own Words*, Mark Putterford (2000, Omnibus Press)
(2) *Metallica: The Frayed Ends Of Metal*, Chris Crocker (1993, St. Martins Griffen Publishing)
(3) *Metallica Unbound: The Unofficial Biography*, K.J. Doughton (1993, Warner Books)

OTHER RECOMMENDATIONS
The Book of Metal, Chris Ingham (2002, Carlton Books)
Fargo Rock City, Chuck Klosterman (2002, Scribner)
Bang Your Head: The Rise and Fall of Heavy Metal, David Konow (2002, Three Rivers Press)

ABOUT THE AUTHOR
Chris Ingham is the Editor of *Metal Hammer UK*, the world's biggest selling monthly metal music magazine. He's also been a lifelong Metallica fan, ever since he was initiated into the family after "liberating" a copy of *Master of Puppets* from a school mate. Subsequent to that incident, which resulted in his first black eye, he spent several of his teenage years with his neck in traction following repeated whiplash while also taking great pride in cultivating the lifelong hatred of his neighbours who failed to appreciate the cathartic qualities of excessive volume.
He now lives in North London with his wife Emma, the devil's own cat, Mr White Feet, and an ever-growing collection of Kiss tat. He can be found online at www.metalhammer.co.uk

THANKS TO
Emma, Tommy Udo (the real hero of the day), Luke for sound advice, and, as ever, the infectious enthusiasm of Mr King.

Printed in Dubai

PICTURE CREDITS

CORBIS
32, 46, NEAL PRESTON 96
GLEN E. FRIEDMAN 14, 29
MICK HUTSON
92, 138, 140/1
MICHAEL JOHANSSON
46, 51, 53, 56/57, 58, 76, 80, 87
LFI
10, 15, 16/17,40/41, 50, 74/75, 84
METAL HAMMER
ANTON CORBIJN 9
REDFERNS
18, 23, 35, 43, 55, 59, 73, 101, 119,
RETNA
4, 21, 36, 45, 63, 68, 71, 79, 111, 115, 123, 124, 126, 128, 130, 131, 133, 135, 136, 106/7, 116/7, 120/1
REX
12, 31, 62
S.I.N
7, 10, 24/5, 27,70, 98 103,

Every effort has been made to acknowledge correctly and contact the source and/or copyright holder of each picture and Carlton Books Limited apologises for any unintentional errors or omissions which will be corrected in future editions of this book.

Nothing Else Matters

METALLICA

The Stories Behind the Biggest Songs

Chris Ingham with Tommy Udo

THUNDER'S MOUTH PRESS

contents

'Like a lot of what James writes, even if you have the lyrics right in front of you, there's still so many possibilities in there. That's the greatest thing about his lyrics.' *Lars Ulrich, 1991*

Introduction

When the big black book of heavy metal is finally written there will be many names vying for the top slot. But one name stands apart as a colossus standing astride millions of album sales, gig tickets and T-shirt sales – Metallica. "Birth. School. Metallica. Death" says one of the band's innumerable T-shirt designs. And it ain't wrong, for as many of you know, once the Metallica bug has sunk its fangs deep into your musical soul there's little turning back.

There's no magic answer to the question of what makes a Metallica song special to millions. It could be the majestic power of their songs, or maybe you were turned on in the early days enslaved by their utter establishment-dismantling fury. Perhaps you were one of the millions wowed by the bombastic "black album", and have stayed faithful ever since, despite the changing nature of their of later material.

Throughout their 20-year career and the many changes to their music, one thing has remained constant in Metallica's world and that is the intensity of James Hetfield. James's contribution to Metallica goes way beyond his duties as a singer, guitarist and frontman in the biggest metal band the world has ever seen. If all that weren't enough, as the only lyricist in the band James has also taken on the mantle of Metallica's keeper of the flame, for it is he alone who puts his thoughts out there for millions to see and judge. We'll punch the air in time to Lars' beats and rake the air alongside James and Kirk's vicious riffs, but its James's lyrics that each one of us connects to. When fans sing the words to "The God That Failed" all but the real hardcore will be unaware that it is a song written about the death of James' mother. To be the lyricist in any band is a tough job, but to be the lyricist in a band as accomplished as Metallica takes serious brass balls.

Chris Ingham, London 2003

Influences

NWOBHM

'I was truly obsessed by the New Wave of British Heavy Metal'

Lars Ulrich, September 1988 (1)

In the early 1980s the young Lars Ulrich was obsessed by a new breed of heavy music. Punk had held sway over British music throughout the latter part of the 1970s, when bands such as The Sex Pistols, The Damned and The Clash replaced old gods Deep Purple, Black Sabbath and Led Zeppelin in the minds of younger music fans. Where once the old guard had been seen to be at the very forefront of contemporary music their extended 20-minute jams were now regarded as self-indulgent, bloated and out of touch. In the popular media of the day, punk swept away the old rockers and battled against the rise of disco before giving way to the more radio-friendly sounds of New Wave. By 1980 bands such as The Jam, Blondie and The Undertones were making regular forays to the top of the British charts.

For its part heavy metal was still a working-class staple, and while its heroes could still command respectable crowds in town halls and theatres it was largely preaching to the converted. Real development in the scene had been driven underground. While more aggressive guitar-led groups such as Judas Priest, Scorpions, UFO and Motörhead had certainly pushed the scene forward, it was in the young working-class pubs and clubs of urban Britain that one had to look for real change.

Fuelled by the speed and passion of punk, but unlike their nose-pierced cousins still mindful and full of respect for the musicianship of the bands that had gone before, this new breed of aggressive guitar acts came to be grouped together under the unwieldy name of the New Wave Of British Heavy Metal.

As a committed anglophile, Lars Ulrich was already a passionate devotee of the likes of Judas Priest and the intensely uncompromising Motörhead. Via the pages of Brit music weekly *Sounds* magazine, he would eagerly devour news of any band credited with being faster or more powerful than the last. As teenagers Lars and Brian Slagel (soon to be the head of hugely influential Metal Blade Records) would meet up every few weeks to pool resources and buy up whatever selection of NWOBHM imports Los Angeles' specialist record stores had shipped in that week.

In the great scheme of things NWOBHM had to have the distinction of being the single most ridiculous acronym one could find, that is until you hear the names of some of the bands that came under its uncompromising moniker: Tygers of Pang Tang, Venom, Ethel The Frog, Tank, Raven, Sledgehammer, Trespass, Sweet Savage, Holocaust, Blitzkreig, Angel Witch, Vardis and Diamond Head, not to mention the scene's three acknowledged leaders – Saxon, Def Leppard and Iron Maiden. Ultimately only Iron Maiden and Def Leppard would stand the test of time, with the former becoming an enduring and widely respected icon in heavy metal circles and the latter, albeit briefly, one of the most popular music artists of the late 1980s.

Angel Witch struck horror into the hearts of fashion gurus everywhere, while their music was the stuff of comedic legend.

Iron Maiden

'They, more than any other band, are responsible for opening up the doors for heavy metal in the 1980s...They've never given in, and as a result have been a big inspiration to a band like us, to stick to what we believe in and not just turn out crap to sell records or please radio stations...'

Lars on Iron Maiden, November 1987 (1.18)

Iron Maiden

A must-buy for young NWOBHM fan Lars Ulrich was the twin-guitar attack of Iron Maiden, who had laid waste to their domestic competition since their emergence from London's notorious East End in 1980. Listening to early Metallica it's easy to assess what drew Ulrich, and later James Hetfield and Cliff Burton, to the Maiden sound. The driving speed of Maiden founder and captain of the ship Steve Harris was reminiscent of another early Metallica hero, UFO's Pete Way, but in the hands of Harris that galloping bass sound was taken to an even more aggressive level.

Perhaps key to Metallica's love of Iron Maiden was the way in which even from their earliest days the Maiden posse have never seen themselves as "just another" heavy metal band, limited to a handful of unimaginative power riffs with a sole aim to drive the listener into a primal fury. There has always been more to Iron Maiden than a riff and a closed fist. From the beginning Steve Harris had conceived of his band as one of imagination unfettered, and as his songwriting grew so did the scope of Maiden's raucous yet still melodic sound. Early fist-punching anthems such as "Running Free" and "Wrathchild" gave way to more complex yet still powerful arrangements like "Prodigal Son", "Purgatory" and "Another Life" that paved the way for the next generation of flamboyant upstarts like Metallica. With the release of 1982's seminal *Number Of The Beast* album the band set down a blueprint for any metal band harbouring arena-sized dreams. Iron Maiden held dearly the belief that on-stage theatrics were an essential ingredient in the projection of their music, and though never likely to rival Alice Cooper or Kiss (with whom they would enjoy a hugely successful European tour in 1980), the band would often spend huge wads of their still-limited budget on flashpots, expensive lighting rigs and the development of their notorious undead mascot Eddie the 'Ead. While Metallica would never go as far as to create their own mascot or theme their covers like Maiden, they were nevertheless sufficiently influenced by the Brit camp to add dramatic theatrics to

their stage show when budget allowed, most notably with their pyro-tastic collapsing Lady Justice statue on the '88–'90 "Damaged Justice" tour and the fake exploding lighting rig routine employed on the "Load" trek.

Metallica's ascension to the top of the metal tree was not nearly as swift as Maiden, who went from East Ham to Madison Square Gardens in a little over three years, but it's safe to say that while the speed freak and power metal fan in Ulrich noted the on-stage theatrics, Hetfield was duly taken by the scope of Maiden's increasingly complex arrangements, especially the band's breakthrough record *Number of The Beast* with classic heavy metal vocalist Bruce Dickinson. Nicknamed "the Air Raid siren", Dickinson's almost classically trained vocals soared above Maiden's ferocious rhythms, even acting as a third guitar on some of the higher wails on "Hallowed Be Thy Name", clearly the forefather to Metallica's classic "Welcome Home (Sanitarium)" from *Master of Puppets*. Indeed, "Hallowed…" wouldn't be the last Maiden song to bear a resemblance to a speeded-up, more complex bastard offspring bearing the Metallica logo, or maybe it is just coincidence that the then biggest metal band in the world would record an Egyptian-themed album in 1984 called *Powerslave* only to see the cheeky young turks in Metallica release an equally catchy Egyptian-themed pit anthem in "Creeping Death" a matter of months later!

Iron Maiden's twin-guitar attack, originally provided by Dave Murray and Dennis Stratton before the more melodic Adrian Smith replaced the latter in 1981, was equally influential on the Metallica sound. From the outset Hetfield and Mustaine would trade solos and riffs in homage to their heroes like Randy Rhodes, Priest's Glen Tipton and KK Downing, and of course Maiden's Murray and Smith. However, with the addition of Kirk Hammett all bets were off as the teen prodigy who tutored under Bay Area guitar legend Joe Satriani would, alongside fellow guitar thrashers Kerry King and Jeff Hanneman of Slayer, rewrite the limits of what a metal solo could or could not be about in the 1980s. With the increasing maturity and proficiency of Hetfield's rhythm playing by the time the Metallica duo recorded *Master of Puppets*, the pair would eclipse any of their mentors' prior glories.

The Misfits

The Misfits crawled out of a New York high school sewer in the late 1970s. Led by the enigmatic frontman Glenn Danzig, The Misfits' ghoulish on-stage persona was one drenched in Hammer horror B-movie theatrics and buffed biceps. Early line-ups changed with every 7" release but always featured Danzig on vocals and Jerry Only on bass before settling on a third permanent member, Only's younger brother Doyle on guitar, in the early Eighties.

Musically, The Misfits were centred on intense three-chord buzzsaw guitar blasts that rarely lasted beyond the two-minute mark. Dumb, dark, loud and fun were the four simple requirements for inclusion into a Misfits mantra. Lyrically, though, The Misfits stood alone: gore, gore and more gore, nothing more. Fifties horror movies provided fertile copy for Danzig's shlock-obsessed mind – "Return of the Fly", "The Horror Business", "50 Eyes", "I Turned Into A Martian" and "Teenagers From Mars" are just some of the stoopid song titles that have made their way into pop culture history.

The Misfits were harmless enough, appealing as they did to the disenfranchised punk rock kid of urban America. However, this is not to say that Danzig and his not-so-merry ghouls had no capacity to outrage – the more morally ambiguous source material for 'Bullet' (President Kennedy's assassination complete with the evocative image of a fellating Jackie O) or Metallica's own favourite Misfits cover, "Last Caress", with the infamous lines of "I got something to say, I killed your baby today/raped your mother today, It doesn't matter much to me as long as it's dead/she's spread" have caused more than a few parents to order the removal of Misfits records from their teenage offspring's collections!

Quite what drew Metallica to The Misfits remains a mystery. There is no doubt that the band were drawn to the energy of the punk outfit's shlock rock approach, and their later decision to cover Brit punks Killing Joke's "The Wait" and, more tellingly, The Anti-Nowhere League's supremely anti-social classic "So What?" ("I've f*cked a pig/I've f*cked a goat/So What? You boring little c*nt!") certainly points to Metallica being a band still determined to piss off the mainstream.

Undoubtedly though, Metallica were metal heads to a man, so the answer as to why The Misfits became such

an obsession may lie with the broader tastes of bassist Cliff Burton. Though the oldest of Metallica by only a year, Burton played a big brother role to the rest and almost certainly benefitted from his own older sibling's diverse record collection.

Never one to join in the crowd Burton was as likely to whip out a Necros 7" single and wax lyrical about its merits as he was some rare Deep Purple bootleg with a 20-minute bass solo. As teens Metallica were record collectors who hunted down European metal imports and were therefore sympathetic to the unique thrill of discovery associated with hardcore fans.

Ultimately Danzig's "evil" Elvis-style vocals lent an atmosphere of the kitsch rather than the threatening, and it was this realization that would lead the highly strung singer to dissolve The Misfits in '83 in order to pursue a more violent slasher-movie-led direction with his new project Samhain. After four years and three albums Danzig would go solo and score minor hits with his dark, blues-tinged biker rock and did indeed go on to support Metallica on the band's hugely successful "Blind Justice" tour of Europe during late 1988.

Diamond Head

Diamond Head were formed in Stourbridge, England, in 1979 by the now-revered (among metal guitarists anyway) Brain Tatler and young singer Sean Harris. Tatler, it was said at the time, couldn't write a bad riff if he tried, and many critics believed that he would go on to rival even Black Sabbath's Tony Iommi in that department.

The band debuted in 1981 with a barnstorming effort called *Lightning To The Nations* and followed it a year later with *Borrowed Time*, picking up a lucrative major label US deal with MCA en route. However, their third album, *Canterbury*, failed to find an audience and a combination of bad label management and too few classic tunes put the dampeners on any lofty ambitions to keep pace with fellow NWOBHM-ers Iron Maiden and Def Leppard all too quickly.

Back from the dead

In 1987, Lars Ulrich headed up a project to compile a Diamond Head retrospective "Best of" called *Behold the Beginning*, and in the sleeve notes comments that without Diamond Head there would've been no hint of a Metallica.

Still a fan at heart, Ulrich was also instrumental in convincing Diamond Head to reform in 1992 and a year later made sure that they held on to the opening slot at a huge Metallica-headlined gig at Milton Keynes, England, in front of 50,000 people.

Facing indifference, Diamond Head disbanded soon after, only to regroup again a few years later to record their much-delayed fourth album, *Death and Progress*, which featured no lesser talents than Tony Iommi and Megadeth's Dave Mustaine in guest mode. Sadly the album failed to have any impact and Diamond once again resigned themselves to their past glories and called it a day.

As often happens in bands with such celebrated lead guitarists, egos battles with the singer were rife, and though Harris and Tatler have often patched up their differences for the sake of the band's momentum it was a case of too little too late.

> 'Listening to their records now is still an inspiration to me...'

Lars Ulrich, talking about Diamond Head in November 1987 (1.18)

Another major influence on Metallica has to be UK riff-merchants Diamond Head. Metallica have covered a number of their songs as B-sides in their time, not least of which is the live favourite "Am I Evil", which made its first appearance alongside another cover version, "Blitzkreig", on the B-side to the "Creeping Death" 12" single under the moniker "Garage Days Revisited" – a cheeky reference to the bygone days of banging out cover tunes in Lars' garage in LA. Listen to "Seek And Destroy" then try Diamond Head's "Dead Reckoning" and see how many similarities you can spot!

Diamond Head pictured in 1981 hanging around the backstreets of decaying Stourbridge. Nice.

Motörhead

'I don't think I can put into words how much Motörhead meant to me when I first started buying their records and going to their gigs. I remember when they supported Ozzy in the States and me and some friends followed their bus around for about six days...'

Lars Ulrich, November, 1987 (1.18)

Motörhead's incomparable frontman Lemmy once quipped that if his band moved in next door to you then your "lawn would die." Remarkably, Motörhead are now into their fourth decade as a touring and recording entity, and there's still no signs of turning down the volume!

Formed out of the ashes of Hawkwind in 1975 by bassist/vocalist and cultural icon Ian "Lemmy" Kilminster, the wayward son of a Welsh firebrand preacher, Motörhead have always subscribed to the doctrine of playing the heaviest blues metal known to man. The band quickly established themselves as the UK band of the moment in the late Seventies with a trio of addictive adrenaline-led albums starting with '78's *Overkill*, '79's *Bomber* and their finest studio outing, *Ace of Spades*, in 1980. Nobody but nobody was making music as loud, dirty or deliberately obnoxious as Lemmy's crew. Indeed, for years Motörhead were the only metal band that it was cool for even hardcore punks to like!

Motörhead's influence on Metallica cannot be overstated – it's more than coincidence that Lars decided upon a double bass drum set-up which was practised at the time by Motörhead's Phil Taylor. Much of

the aesthetic that the young Metallica were striving to capture as they recorded *Kill 'Em All* is exactly the 'Head spirit that had imprinted itself upon them after they had long worn out their old vinyl copies of *No Sleep 'Til Hammersmith*. Indeed, it's virtually impossible to listen to early Metallica songs such as "Motorbreath" (a direct tribute by any other name!), "Phantom Lord" or "Metal Militia" and not hear the thrashing bass chords and pummelling double bass drum beats of "Overkill", "Iron Horse" or "Stone Deaf Forever".

At Lemmy's 50th birthday bash held at the Rainbow club on Sunset Boulevard, Hollywood in 1995, the Metallica posse climbed into identical black shirts/jeans and stuck on Lemmy-style sideburns and moustaches to take to the stage as "the Lemmys," where they performed a short but hilarious six-song set

of 'Head classics (which they were to subsequently record and release as a limited-edition EP called *Metallihead* in '96).

Motörhead's no-holds-barred, no-frills metal played at obscene volume turned many a young European's head on to the power of heavy metal music, but none more so than Copenhagen-born Lars Ulrich. Indeed, Lars would regularly spend his college vacations and breaks from sports school following Motörhead around Europe as they toured, and would subsequently religiously see every one of the band's Californian shows whenever they made one of their rare appearances in the US. As Lars told the BBC: 'What we got from Motörhead in '81 was the aggression and the energy and the speed that they had back then, around the *Overkill* and *Ace Of Spades* albums...' (2.24)

Venom •

Like all bands Motörhead made many a line-up change, first losing "Fast" Eddie Clark in 1983 to ex-Thin Lizzy man Brian Robertson for the *Another Perfect Day* record, before ditching him and switching to a two-guitar line-up with Phil Campbell and Wurzel for the new tracks on the 1985 "Best Of" compilation, which was to stand for the next ten years. Long-time drummer "Philthy" Phil Taylor was to drop in and out of the band throughout the late Eighties until ex-King Diamond powerhouse Mikkey Dee joined them to add a new lease of life in the early Nineties. Since 1995 Motörhead have held on to their classic three-piece line-up, having dumped Wurzel following the recording of '95's *Sacrifice* album.

Lemmy complains bitterly that people don't respect Motörhead's newer songs while the band have been producing some of the most consistent material of their careers over the last five years with records such as *Overnight Sensation* [1998], *We Are Motörhead* [2001] and *25 Alive* [2001]. Having said that, 2002's hastily thrown together album, *Hammered*, pushed the band straight back to square one in terms of their new material competing with "classic" Lemmy-Clarke-Taylor sets, much to the singer's chagrin.

'I know people regard *Kill 'Em All* as the start of thrash, but I give full credit to Venom. They started it all. Their first album, *Welcome To Hell*, was so fucking unique when it first hit. And Metallica were obviously heavily influenced by them.' Lars Ulrich (1.18)

Venom charged out of the economically ruined wastes of northern England with their 1981 debut *Welcome To Hell*. Musically, Venom were influenced by many of the NWOBHM bands but theatrically they took the "satan" angle much further, coining the phrase "Black Metal" for the title of their second album in 1982.

No angle was left unturned in the search for the shock value at their hands, from the band's stage names, allegedly demon titles taken straight from the pages of the Necronomicon – Abaddon (drums), Cronos (bass/vocals), Mantas (guitars) – to their dry ice and laser/pyro-filled stage shows. Talking about their OTT image, motormouth vocalist Cronos cited Venom as having: "Exactly what Kiss lacked! You look at Gene Simmons – and he was a 'demon!' And there's fire and death and he stands there going, 'I was made for loving you baby!' And you say what the f*cking hell is this?"

Venom promised that they "sat at Lord Satan's left hand", the cover of *Welcome To Hell* featured a goat's head pentagram while *Black Metal* had a picture of the Horned One himself, though it's highly unlikely that the band had any serious affiliation with the religion. Despite initial breakthroughs Venom failed to develop their ultra-aggressive stance over subsequent records, and many of the bands that they influenced would overtake them in the credibility stakes, not least of which were Metallica.

As the 1980s progressed the band issued two more similar-sounding records, '84's *At War With Satan* and '85's *Possessed*, before line-up changes robbed them of any identity – Mantas left first, only to rejoin two years later at Cronos's expense. Venom soldiered on with a variety of personnel and albums until the early Nineties when Abaddon, by now the only remaining original member, put the band on hold.

A reformation of the original line-up occurred in 1998, and though it created significant interest in mainland Europe, where Venom remain a powerful draw on the metal festival circuit, the larger UK market and the US remains nonplussed.

These days Venom are content to play the Euro circuit and milk their legacy as the founders of black metal, leaving young pups like Cradle of Filth, Mayhem, Dimmu Borgir and Satyricon to play the shock crowd card.

Formation

Given Lars Ulrich's lifetime passion for all things heavy metal, it was probably inevitable that he would seek an outlet to become just like his wild-maned heroes. Having grown up in the international tennis-playing world due to his father Torben's success, Lars felt obligated to pursue sports fame. One visit to a Deep Purple concert as an impressionable 10-year-old changed all that, and soon the tennis racket had been swapped for upturned pots of paint and 'drumsticks' as Lars banged out "Smoke On The Water" for the umpteenth time before breakfast. It's entirely possible that Lars more or less escaped to the world of heavy metal as a stress reliever from the pressures of his own burgeoning tennis-playing regime. But whatever the truth, by the time he hit his mid-teens young Ulrich was an avid devourer of all things bearing umlauts and loud guitars. Having followed every European metal band around California whenever they came to play, Lars grew tired of waiting for them to arrive and spent the summer of 1981 camped in England chasing down his favourite bands in their rehearsal rooms – Lars famously even blagged his way into Motörhead's inner sanctum as they prepared material for what would become the *Iron Fist* album! Being around such acts as Motörhead, Diamond Head, Jaguar and others fed Lars' dream of doing it all himself, and upon returning to LA he felt like a man on a mission.

Prior to leaving for England Lars had already hooked up with Phantom Lord, who featured Ron McGovney on bass, Hugh Tanner on lead guitar and one James Hetfield on rhythm, for an all-too-brief jam session.

At the time Hetfield existed on the fringes of Lars' euro-metal clique – they shared a mutual friend in the metal-obsessed Brian Slagel – and Lars would later claim that before they hooked up the only real metal band that James had ever heard of was Iron Maiden. James' elder brother, David, was an avid classic rock fan and had long instilled the benefits of Sabbath, Skynyrd, AC/DC, Deep Purple and Aerosmith into his younger sibling's soul and so Ulrich and Hetfield still had much to babble about. As the son of committed Christian Scientist parents, Hetfield had a sober, thoroughly working-class upbringing, so the attraction of hanging out with the outgoing well-travelled Ulrich and all his metal leanings was more than tempting.

When Lars returned from Europe at the end of summer '81, he and Hetfield, who had used the break from Lars to play in a local garage band called Leather Charm with his friend and housemate Ron McGovney, rekindled their jamming sessions and eagerly started looking for additional members. McGovney was drafted onto bass and an extended network of metal friends yielded up Lloyd Grant, who as a metal-mad black guitarist was a rare sight on the LA scene.

It's credited that the first song Lars and James ever wrote together was "Hit The Lights" in James's front room "rehearsal space", but in actual fact the song was little more than a re-working of an earlier Leather Charm song. Why the rush? Lars' longtime friend Brian Slagel had taken a job at a local record distribution company, and was busily putting his newly acquired record contacts into practice for the LA scene. Devising a compilation album called *Metal Massacre* for all the new LA bands he was in contact with, Slagel offered a slot to his buddy Lars. It gave Lars and co something to aim for even if they hadn't yet come up with a name. Though the trio advertised, no one of quality came forward and a disheartened McGovney initially quit the project. Instead James recorded all the guitar, bass and vocal tracks separately, with Lars on drums. Still searching for the lead guitarist, an ad in *Recycler* yielded up ex-Panic guitarist Dave Mustaine, a blond, flashy motormouth of a teenager. Mustaine recorded a seering lead break for "Hit The Lights" but still the Ulrich/Hetfield axis were unhappy, and bizarrely asked Jamaican born Lloyd Grant to record a second break for the demo. "Lloyd could play leads like a muthafucker," remembers James, "but his rhythm stuff was never very tight" (3.22). Although sometimes listed as an early Metalli-member, Grant's only contribution to the band was the ten-second lead break on "Hit The Lights".

Another network friend – San Francisco's Ron Quintana – was considering titles for a metal fanzine (*Metal Mania* as it became known) and benignly offered his well-thought-out list to Ulrich for inspection. Never one to miss a trick, Lars pointed the hapless scribe away from one name on the shortlist and phoned to tell the rest of the guys that he had found a name for their project – Metallica. Soon after, and without ever even having performed a live gig, Metallica handed Slagel the demo of "Hit The Lights", and alongside the debut recording by Ratt, it turned out to be one of the stand-out tracks on that first *Metal Massacre* record released in June 1982. (Original pressings misspell the name as Mettalica, and the band duly re-recorded the track with Mustaine on all leads and McGovney on bass for the subsequent re-pressing!) At the time, though, *Metal Massacre* caused enough interest to become a popular series upon which metal fans could rely to discover the most exciting new sounds of the day.

A huge euro metal-o-phile like James and Lars, Mustaine initially seemed to fit like a glove and alongside a re-recruited McGovney it was this line-up – with James concentrating solely on vocals – that made a debut outing under the Metallica name on March 14, 1982, at Radio City in Anaheim.

It was an awkward affair for the fledgling metal heads as Mustaine broke a string on the opening number, "Hit The Lights". Recalls James: "There was no experience there. We didn't know what to do. Tell a joke? We learned a lot from that gig though. I don't think anyone from the band had gotten up on the stage before and played. Maybe Dave, in his previous band, but I know Lars hadn't. I had played a couple of parties, but I don't think Ron had played before, either. Everyone was pretty fuckin' new, very green on that stage!" (3.23).

Two weeks later and Lars had blagged the band the opening slot to cult UK metallers Saxon's two shows at the Whisky on Sunset Strip.

Remembers Brian Slagel of that first support moment: "James didn't even play guitar – Mustaine was the only guitar player on stage. Their set basically consisted of Diamond Head covers and a couple of other NWOBHM numbers. I think 'Hit The Lights' was the only original song that they performed. They were essentially a garage band at the time" (2.29).

The search for the ideal rhythm player proved fruitless as the guys who tried were either in too much competition with the fiery Mustaine (not a good idea) or too sloppy for the powerful aggressive sound Metallica were after. After trying out a gig in April with Brad Parker on second guitar as a five-piece band, which

didn't work out, and after considerable prompting by Lars, James reluctantly agreed to partner Mustaine and take on the singing duties as well.

However, Metallica's furious almost punk-like speed – a perception further enhanced by Hetfield's punkish screeching style of vocal – proved a challenge for the local LA crowds. Metallica were simply too raucous, aggressive and underground for the LA metal clubs yet their long hair, lead breaks and obvious metal world-view was equally as alien to the hardcore clubs kicking out tunes by the likes of Black Flag, The Germs and Bad Religion.

Spurred on by the support of friends the band committed to a making a demo tape of their new material – legend actually has it that the ever-pushy Lars approached Brian Slagel for something like eight thousand dollars to record an album before modifying his expectations. *No Life 'Til Leather* featured a re-recorded "Hit The Lights", "Seek and Destroy", "Motorbreath", "The Four Horsemen", "Jump In The Fire", "Phantom Lord" and "Metal Militia". The metal world was never the same again.

Formation pt 2: the scene

At the time of Metallica's first album in 1983 the US rock and metal scene was largely ruled by the West Coast party metal bands like Van Halen, the recently unmasked Kiss, Quiet Riot and the indomitable Ozzy Osbourne, plus upcoming establishment-baiting shock rockers such as WASP and Mötley. By mid-'83, Metallica had been a "band" for over two years and their *No Life 'Til Leather* demo had made significant international impact on the fledgling underground tape trading scene. However, Metallica's hometown of LA had little time for a bunch of scraggy, acne-ridden metal heads obsessed with Motörhead. When Metallica managed to play hometown shows they were invariably booked third on the bill to the likes of Steeler, Dokken and Ratt. "We gigged around LA for a year and a half – very unsuccessfully!" remembers Lars (1). "The city never really took to us … things just never worked out." The reticence of the City of Angels to take Metallica to its bosom meant that the band travelled to where the crowds did love them – San Francisco.

The Stone venue had a reputation for booking all manner of LA bands, but its crowds were particularly fond of those with a more European, thrashier, heavier feel. Exactly what Metallica had to offer. As Lars remembered in the *New York Daily News* years later: "Everyone in LA was too worried about spilling their drink and looking around to see who else was in the club. Up in San Francisco, the kids were more open minded and more down to earth. They didn't care what anyone else thought" (2.38).

Adds James: "San Francisco was our first encounter with real fans. It was like, these people are here for us, and they like us, and they hate the other bands – and we like that 'cause we hate 'em too. These people appreciated us for our music, and not because of how we looked, which was how LA was." (3.31).

Indeed, the band were so blown away by San Fran's love for them that they immortalized their show at the Waldorf on November 29 when they recorded the *Live Metal Up Your Ass* demo tape purely for the local Metalli-fans.

It was on one of the jaunts to San Francisco in the fall of 1982 that Brian Slagel came across Cliff Burton, the bass player of a local band called Trauma whom he was looking at placing on Vol. 2 of *Metal Massacre*. Slagel was blown away by Burton, and when Lars later phoned to bitch about Ron McGovney's lack of commitment to Metallica, Slagel urged the Metallica guys to check Burton out as Trauma were due to play the Whisky very soon.

With a wild, freestyle approach to playing, Burton's whipping basslines and sheer on-stage panache simply bowled the Metallica crew over on first look. James and Lars each knew that they had to have the bassist in Metallica – only Cliff wasn't budging to LA. After some four months of constant battling James, Lars and even the risible Dave took a long look at LA's apathetic reaction to Metallica and how it compared to the burgeoning scene in San Francisco and the presence of their desired bass player, and agreed to decamp further north – if Cliff would have them.

"The first time we jammed with Cliff, I wanted to ram through the fuckin' wall," recalled James to Ron Quintana's fanzine a few months later. "He blew my mind. He fits like a glove."

Added Dave Mustaine: "His solos are fantastic. They've got Bach and Beethoven in them as well as rock, metal, and some Pink Floyd-type shit. Cliff's bad ass."

Bad ass he may have been, but added to that list has to be: driven, determined, inspirational, experimental and sheer bloody mental! Cliff Burton radically altered the songwriting chemistry of Metallica and ultimately it would be he who would push the band to their creative max.

A fresh-faced James Hetfield salutes the front-row faithful at an early Metallica gig.

The trouble with Dave

Dave Mustaine is undoubtedly one of the finest metal musicians of his generation. When it comes to speed guitar, technical ecstasy and dry, savage wit, no one comes close to the glory years of Mustaine's Megadeth. But for many years there was a dark side to Dave, one that would emerge whenever alcohol reared its head – and in the early daze of Metallica alcohol was an ever-present ally-cum-foe.

No single reason has ever emerged as to why the co-writer on some of Metallica's flashiest early tunes was given the boot, but it does seem clear that James and Lars gave Dave more than what they considered to be enough chances to get with the Metallica program. Stories abound that Mustaine kicked Hetfield's dog at a party resulting in a punch-up between the two, another that having already heard the young Kirk Hammett's breaks on a recent Exodus demo tape Hetfield remained unimpressed by Mustaine's lead breaks and felt that they added nothing to Metallica. Whatever the real reason for Dave's ejection, it all came to a head on April 11, 1983, following a short East Coast jaunt with Vanderburg and The Rods that had been organized by manager Johnny Zazula, when the band asked Dave to leave, handing him a ticket for a Greyhound bus that departed in two short hours. It was a particularly painful blow as the band were out on the East Coast readying themselves to record their debut album. A record on which many of Mustaine's songs would appear even if his lead breaks would not.

In an interview with *Metal Mania* fanzine shortly afterwards Lars recalled a particular incident that crystallized all their fears about Dave:

"We were driving along in the U-haul 'limo', having a wonderful time sleeping in the back and shit, when we ran into problems around Iowa involving a drug called 'Alcohol & Dave'. Dave got really drunk. He'd probably had 15 or 20 beers and was driving the truck while we were crashed out in the back – he almost killed us 15 or 20 times! About 7 o'clock that night we stopped to eat, and Dave and [tour manager and Exodus manager] Mark Whittaker got into a huge fight. Everyone was sober except Dave, and after a while, he passed out in the back. The four of us were in the front, talking about how this guy isn't stable enough to be happening on the road. He's a great guy and a great friend, but he just couldn't handle his alcohol. So that night, just out of Chicago, we shook hands and decided that this was the end, and that we'd get Kirk" (3.40).

Jason Newsted (left) replaced Cliff Burton, Kirk Hammett (right) replaced Dave Mustaine – but the drummer remained the same.

Kirk Hammett: the final piece of the puzzle

When James Hetfield and Lars Ulrich first heard Kirk Hammett play his lead breaks on Exodus's classic 1981 demo tape featuring "Death And Domination", "Whipping Queen" and "Warlords", they knew they were listening to the sound of a guitarist they wanted. As Bay Area natives Exodus were extremely well known to the Metallica camp, a situation compounded by the fact that

their tour manager and house mate in SF, Mark Whitaker, was Exodus's "sometime" manager. It's highly likely that any simmering tension between the Hetfield/Ulrich axis and Mustaine throughout 1982 was being fed by the frustrating realization that having already recruited the hottest bassist from the Bay Area in the form of Cliff Burton, at their fingertips – but strictly off limits – remained the most talented guitar prospect to emerge in years. Crucially, when Metallica reached breaking point and made the decision, they didn't fire Mustaine and hope to hold auditions, they fired their friend already knowing that Hammett had a plane ticket in his pocket and was on his way out to record the lead breaks on what would be Metallica's debut record. By the time Mustaine had completed his slow three-day journey across America back to SF, Kirk Hammett had already landed in New York and was rehearsing material with the band at Johnny Zazula's house.

Metallica, however, were simply ecstatic, at Mustaine's obvious expense, having now poached Hammett from Exodus. As James gushed praise in *Whiplash* fanzine soon after: "Kirk's got Dave's speed, but Dave was all speed. He had no feeling, he had no pull offs, he had no brilliant things. He tried to get brilliant sometimes but it would sound awful." (3.42)

Added Lars: "I'll tell ya, this guy Kirk, he wakes up in the morning and he just plays – I mean all the time. Dave would only play when he wanted to. It wasn't like he played guitar because he wanted to. It was more an excuse to show off" (3.42).

But Dave was gone and Kirk was in. The real Metallica was born.

Enter Megadeth

'Basically, when they told me to leave I was packed in about 20 seconds and I was gone.'

Dave Mustaine on the split, June '86

'Every time I get a magazine that says "Megadeth" on the cover that's the first thing I always turn to, "Let's see what Dave has to say today. Let's see how he can put his size 11s in his mouth once again!"'

Lars on Dave, September '91

The 1983 split from Metallica had been a bitter pill for lead guitarist Mustaine to swallow. The band had grown weary of his irrational temper and alcohol-fuelled rants, and now, facing considerable time in a studio to record their debut album after one drunken argument too many, the rest of the band gave Mustaine his marching orders. It took Dave Mustaine nearly 10 years to forgive his former friends that decision.

By 1984, Mustaine had gone on to form the second biggest band of the thrash scene: Megadeth. More LA-based than Metallica but now trailing his former comrades by a good two years, Mustaine would nevertheless record some of the most technically proficient and furiously celebrated music of the entire thrash scene. Megadeth's sophomore 1986 release, *Peace Sells...But Who's Buying?*, is an acknowledged classic. Yet wracked by drug abuse the 'Deth camp would disintegrate at the end of each album/tour, only to re-emerge seemingly even more pissed off and energized than before!

The *So Far So Good...So What!* album, released in 1987, scored the band a minor hit with a cover of the Pistols' 'Anarchy in The UK', but it was Mustaine's six-minute ode to the recently deceased Cliff Burton called "In My Darkest Hour" that was the true centre of the record with its dense riffing and distressed lyrical content.

However, despite the success of both camps there was forever a simmering feud between Metallica and Megadeth, largely fuelled, it must be said, by the ever-bitchy UK rock press and Mustaine's drug-induced rants. Megadeth even went as far as to re-record one of Mustaine's early Metallica classics – "The Four Horsemen" – under its original name "The Mechanix" for the band's debut 1985 album, *Killing Is My Business...And Business Is Good!*, speeding the track up just that crucial bit in a moment of childish pique and obvious posturing. What is beyond dispute though, is that Metallica continued to use riffs that Mustaine had worked on during his tenure in the band.

Dave shared co-writes on four tracks on *Kill 'Em All* ("The Four Horsemen", "Jump In The Fire", "Phantom Lord" and "Metal Militia"), two on *Ride the Lightning* (the title track and "Call of Ktulu") and, he would argue, was even owed one for "Leper Messiah" on *Master of Puppets*, though the 'Tallica camp have long disputed this.

Whatever the actual truth, Mustaine's contribution to the early Metallica sound should not go understated, and the band's decision to fire him must still rank as one of the most pivotal Metallica have ever made. Without it they would surely have disintegrated amid infighting or James Hetfield would have quit. Instead Metallica marched on to once seemingly impossible glories, and with their countless gold and platinum discs Megadeth didn't exactly do bad either!

The two warring parties made up in 1993 when, at Metallica's behest, Megadeth were asked to be the support at Metallica's huge bash at Milton Keynes Bowl in the UK. Said Lars at the time, "We realized it would be cool to see Dave on the same bill as us...well, we knew it would either be shit or lay the whole thing to rest, anyway."

The lion-maned Mustaine in full view.

The Big Four

'I think that our first album certainly fits into the thrash category, everything going at 500mph. But you can't call songs like "Call of Ktulu" thrash metal. We do play very fast but I think there's more to our songs than just thrashing – we try and arrange them with good breaks, tempo changes and choruses with melody lines.'

Lars, December 1984 (1)

While Metallica clearly spearheaded what became known as the thrash metal movement of the 1980s, like any "leader" the band refused to acknowledge any real kinship with the other bands. To do so of course would have been a risky business, for the band would then only be seen as strong as the scene's weakest link – and in the mid-1980s thrash scene there were a lot of weak links. However, there were several factors that inextricably linked Metallica to the thrash scene. Firstly, though native LA people, the band decamped to San Francisco in late '82 because the scene there supported the band way more than than Los Angeles. Centred around the legendary Stone club Metallica would regularly pack out week nights, and then the more popular weekend nights usually reserved for the more high-profile national touring outfits. Other San Francisco bands would support them,

Opposite: Megadeth's Dave Mustaine shows off his twin-necked mettle.
This page: Slayer's Kerry King always had trouble with airport security when on tour.

the most notable of which was Exodus, who featured a young guitarist called Kirk Hammett whom Metallica would poach when things went awry with Dave Mustaine before the recording of *Kill 'Em All*. Undeterred by Hammett's defection, Exodus would go on to record *Bonded By Blood*, an album arguably as seminal as Metallica's and one every bit as brutal (if not more so!) than *Kill 'Em All*.

While Mustaine would go on to form Megadeth there were still many other young bands making a considerable noise at the time. Foremost of these lived down the West coast in Huntingdon Beach, CA, and they went under the name Slayer. Still going strong some 22 years after their conception in Kerry King's garage as testosterone-led teenagers, Slayer are one band that Metallica give wary respect to – even if it isn't always reciprocated!

Slayer's early years were defined by their simple desire to outpace everything and every band that had gone before – it was Judas Priest and Iron Maiden taken to their musical extremes crossed with a hardcore punk ethic. Decked out in spikes, studded leather and heavy black eye make-up Slayer, even upon release of their 1984 debut album *Show No Mercy*, were initially considered as little more than a joke. That is until their technical genius and savage songwriting began to make considerable waves. Released in 1985, *Hell Awaits* was hardly groundbreaking, but the band began to provoke questions of what would happen should they hook up with a producer who could bring out the best in them. That shape appeared in 1986 in the guise of former Beastie Boys producer Rick Rubin, who overnight harnessed the diabolical power contained within Slayer for the classic *Reign In Blood* album. Clocking in under 26 minutes, *Reign...* is an undisputed heavyweight champion of extreme music. But it also pointed to the ceiling limits of what a band trading on fast music could actually achieve. If the goal of the thrash movement was to create the most extreme yet still listenable record, then it was game over – Slayer had won. Maybe for many thrash bands, that had been their one and only goal, but not so Metallica. For them speed had been a means to an end – an easy way to give an adrenaline shot to catchy, but hardly original, riffs. By 1986 James Hetfield's

songwriting and arrangements had clearly eclipsed those of any band in the thrash scene. Striking as songs such as "Angel of Death" and "Necrophobic" are, they hardly compare to the sheer complexity and delivery of "Master of Puppets", "Disposable Heroes" or even Metallica's own 1986 nod to the old school, "Damage Inc."

The last of the so-called Big Four thrash acts were East Coast-based jokers Anthrax. Metallica and Anthrax shared considerable early history. When the fledgling Metallica finally made it to New York to play off the back of their *No Life 'Til Leather* demo they found small store owners Jon and Marsha Zazula waiting to greet them. The Zazulas looked after one other local band, Anthrax, and when Metallica were invited back to live in the new managers' house the two bands would hang out on a daily basis. When the combined work/home thing became too much it was into Anthrax's rehearsal space that the Metallica guys would move their worldly possessions, and the two bands would regularly practise in rooms next to each other. Indeed if you look at the inside sleeve pic to *Kill 'Em All*, which features Hetfield legs astride and Flying V pumped for action, you will see Kiss logos sprayed across the monitors in front of the singer. If you look that bit closer again you will also notice the word Anthrax dropped beneath it – and that's because Metallica, whenever they played a New York show, would of course borrow Anthrax's gear. When Metallica started to take off in Europe in the mid-Eighties it was Anthrax who would follow them as an official support act – an act of generosity and respect that Anthrax were careful to pass on to any of their own support bands from then on.

At one point, following the release of 1987's *Among The Living* opus, it did seem that Anthrax were destined to enjoy second place and a long, healthy career, tucked in behind the Metallica guys at the forefront of the new breed of heavy metal kings. Where the pre-Bob Rock-era Metallica were moving toward increasingly more complex arrangements, Anthrax were more about creating a vibe in a live crowd. Honed to perfection as a live unit by constant touring around the New York area clubs, Anthrax were a devastating act to follow. The band's tight, crunchy, fast-paced thrash salvos were packed with trash-talking pop culture references and general teenage

Influences

nonsense that appealed the world over. However, the one thing that escaped Anthrax and the one thing that Metallica, Megadeth and certainly Slayer earned, was unyielding fan respect and ultimately, therefore, any lasting credibility.

A series of bad business moves and, it must be said, patchy albums, such as 1988's *State of Euphoria* and 1990's much darker *Persistence of Time*, failed to produce the sales the band were looking for. Unlike Metallica, success for Anthrax would take far longer. Also, unlike any other extreme metal band, Anthrax were prone to having a laugh at their own expense. "Joke" moments such as the ill-advised "I'm the Man" single (which lampooned the Beastie Boys and the band's constant use of *Mad* magazine cartoon imagery and "street" slang-cum-pop culture terms ("Not", "mosh" etc) made them easy targets.

Unfortunately, when the music quality started to slip due to the intense writing/recording/touring pressures that the band put themselves through, Anthrax found that there was no hardcore fanbase on whom they could rely.

That said, with a change of singer Anthrax still produced the best album of their career in the shape of 1993's *Sound of White Noise* with former Armoured Saint man John Bush leading the way. Ironically, Bush was once considered by Metallica for a lead vocalist slot when the band were about to record *Ride the Lightning*. At the time James Hetfield had become unsure over the quality of his vocals and whether he could possibly keep up the singing/guitar combination night after night on tour, now that Metallica were becoming an in-demand international act. Rather famously, Bush actually turned Metallica down(!) to stay with his original outfit, believing them to be a flash-in-the-pan and that they wouldn't get anywhere. Oops.

By the mid-Nineties, Anthrax were plagued by bad record companies and bad management as they limped from label to label, frustrated by a lack of career momentum, though occasionally taking advantage of beneficial support slots from younger acts like Pantera who still consider them an influence.

Anthrax ham it up. As usual.

2

Kill 'em All

Behind the scenes

Martin Hooker and his business partner Gem Howard were instrumental figures in the initial success of Metallica. Given the band's early ferocious sound it was quite apparent that Metallica would have a limited audience in the US as long as AOR and big-hair bands like Mötley Crüe, Ratt and Bon Jovi ruled the roost. A decision was taken very early in the band's career by then manager Johnny Z, in agreement with the rest of the Metalli-mob, that the band should exploit overseas markets as early as they could, particularly Europe, where it was considered tastes in rock and metal were naturally harder. To that end, Johnny Z hooked up with Martin and Gem on Martin's fledgling record label Music For Nations. Over the next four years the label would essentially keep Metallica alive on the road until a major label deal with Elektra in the States put the band into the big league.

Martin Hooker: "At the time we started MFN the metal scene was all about NWOBHM, and every label going large or small was looking to sign British metal bands. If MFN was going to be different to the rest then we had look elsewhere. So coming from the punk scene we'd always been close to that underground tape-trading network, so I s'pose it was inevitable that somewhere along the line I'd get sent a copy of the *No Life 'Til Leather* demo. I loved it on first listen. By the time I heard it Johnny Z had already hooked up with Metallica and had his deal in place for North America, but I came along and MFN was able to put a deal into place for *Kill 'Em All*.

"It was one of the most extreme records of its kind for the times. I clearly remember friends of mine back from my EMI days prior to Secret Records hearing the tape and looking incredulously at me saying, 'What are you getting yourself into – this is just noise!' I think the industry assumed we were just going back to our punk roots again only trying to take it one step further.

"The picture on the back of *Kill 'Em All* says it all

about who the band were at the time – spotty, greasy-looking metal heads!"

Gem Howard: "When we released *Kill 'Em All* we shipped only 1,500 copies – that's across the whole of Europe. This was no out-of-the-box success story. I remember the debates as to whether we should bother to press up another 500 copies in 1983."

Martin: "Most people just couldn't get their heads around Metallica at all. They just thought that it was too extreme – you must remember that the biggest metal bands of the day were Iron Maiden and Whitesnake, so early Metallica with its punk roots was a real shock to the system."

Gem: "We brought them over to support Venom and again with Twisted Sister who were the only non-NWOBHM bands doing any real business in England. We actually tried to book in a tour with The Rods and Exciter for Metallica, but even though The Rods were selling quite a lot of records at the time the bill simply failed to sell. I think they sold only 40 tickets at Hammersmith Odeon before they pulled the tour."

Martin: "What were my first impressions of them as people? I think it was, 'Wow, can't Lars talk!?' That said, he's every publicist's dream and every band should have one because he gets so much done it's untrue. James and Kirk were very quiet at the time, still finding their feet, but with Lars around I can understand why they had a back seat. Which left the space cadet – Cliff. You'd look at him and think, 'You just can't be in the right band.' Standing there wearing loon pants and flares and tie-dyed shirts."

What were your first impressions of James?
Martin: "He came across as very shy as if he didn't have a lot to say for himself at all but that might have been because he could never get a word in edgeways with Lars around. I also think that he was withdrawn

because he had very bad skin at the time and it made him very self-conscious."

Gem: "That lack of self-confidence by James seeped over to his performances as well, because right the way through that entire *Ride...* period he still wasn't convinced that he was a good enough guitarist, and he certainly didn't believe that he ought to be the singer in Metallica. Thing is, when people sing their own songs the emotion they'll give out is always going to be far more heartfelt if they are their own lyrics, no matter how technically accomplished they are. James really wanted John Bush from Armoured Saint to do the job instead, but the others – in fact everyone else surrounding Metallica – were telling him otherwise. In the end I think that the success of *Ride...* as a record and the success of the touring that went with it gave James that much-needed confidence booster."

Martin: "When Metallica started shifting those records it really must have made the old guard metal bands sit up and take note. I bet Judas Priest, The Scorpions and Maiden caught a cold listening to that sound."

Martin: "We had an enormous problem in the early days getting the market to understand what Metallica were about. They had long hair and denim jackets so they must be metallers, but they played songs way faster than even Motörhead and sounded like punks. So they were too metal for punks and too punk for metal. It was a real headache in the early days for *Kill 'Em All*. Thankfully I think people just decided they didn't care what it was called – New Wave Of American Heavy Metal Punk NWOAHMP? – they were gonna love it anyway!"

The fledgling Metallica: mulletts, bum fluff 'tache and acne – the not-so-wise monkeys.

Kill 'em All (1983) ●

'We didn't know anything about producing or any of that crap, so the whole thing was kind of innocent. A kind of innocence that you can never recapture after your first time in a studio. I remember [that] they wouldn't let us in the studio to hear any of the mixes…I remember hearing the album and going, "Oh my God, that sucks!" '

James Hetfield, 1992 (1.21)

'*Kill 'Em All* was basically the first ten songs we'd written. What's the point of writing a song that's not good enough to make your record? It ended up sounding very different to anything that had come out of America. We weren't consciously trying to start anything, we were just doing what came naturally.'

Lars Ulrich, 1993 (1.22)

Hetfield's joy at finally getting an album out.

Recorded at Rochester, NY, Music America Studios in April/May '83 at a cost of only $12,000, it may not have been a conscious attempt to change the world, but the sounds unleashed on Metallica's debut *Kill 'Em All* surely changed the face of heavy metal music for generations to come. The sheer fury of the guitars as they stabbed and chopped their way through Hetfield's impassioned shrieks sounded unlike anything that had made its way out of America. Even by NWOBHM standards the only two acts that could match the Metallica fury for speed were Motörhead – a metalled-up blues band by any other name – and the overly theatrical Venom. But even those two giants of the European metal scene couldn't match the sheer balls on display in the Metallica camp, where time changes and brazen riffs were casually thrown the listener's way as if there was an inexhaustible well of such hooks upon which they could draw. As for a bass solo? On a debut record? Now surely someone, somewhere, had to be having a laugh? Yup, someone called Metallica – hell-bent on playing the game their way.

Hit the Lights

A pure Hetfield/Ulrich composition "Hit The Lights" bears the same "metal is the message" theme that many an early Metallica lyric called for. At this stage in their careers Lars and James didn't do much else except tour, drink and bullshit each other in the back of a van, so it's highly appropriate that their initial outpourings would celebrate this metal vagabond lifestyle. Reminiscent of the bombastic intro to an early Iron Maiden classic instrumental called "Genghis Khan" from 1981's *Killers* album, for all its obvious lyrical shortcomings "Hit The Lights" does illustrate the band's clear desire to move ahead of any chasing "thrash" pack. Starting as it does with ascending, aspiring power chords and powerful battering ram-like drum beats as an introduction to Metallica, "Hit The Lights" set the scene nicely, allowing Hetfield's chopping rhythm riffs to come slicing in and tear the listener's skin from their ears in surprise.

The song's live-for-the-day/party-hard theme clearly worked for Motörhead on "(We Are) The Road Crew" so why would it be any less effective for Metallica? It sums up not only the awkward, immature feelings of young, aggressive males readying themselves for the tribal ritual, but also those of the bedroom fan. "Hit The Lights" was written in the earliest days of Metallica, after all it was only two years before its vinyl debut that Lars and James were nothing more than bedroom fans themselves, who had graduated to the heady heights of a fully fledged garage band. The pair's interpretation of what was and was not "cool" remained steeped in perceived messages from the album sleeves and lyrics of such classic metal albums as Motörhead's *No Sleep 'Til Hammersmith* and Diamond Head's *Lightning To The Nations*. "Hit The Lights" is surely an anthem written in anticipation of the nights and for the fans to come, and could easily have been named simply "Metallica" in the way it defines that early metal-'til-I-die ethos that the band were living. Like Iron Maiden and Motörhead's self-titled anthems from their debut records, "Hit The Lights" is Metallica at their stripped-down, cocksure, aggressive best.

The Four Horsemen

Originally titled "The Mechanics" when Dave Mustaine wrote it for the *No Life 'Til Leather* demo (and, as mentioned before, later changed to "The Mechanix" on Megadeth's debut record *Killing Is My Business...And Business is Good!*), "The Four Horsemen" was also expanded by James and Lars musically in the song's middle section as well as featuring completely re-worked lyrics to the original. Given that "The Mechanics" was a Mustaine original and that Dave was fired a matter of days before the band hit the studio to record the album, it clearly didn't leave Hetfield much time to come up with lyrics. No doubt the galloping central riff inspired the charging on horseback theme, or perhaps the apocalyptic visions of the four horsemen had been kicking around Hetfield's mind just waiting for a suitable song to attach to.

Though James Hetfield in particular would later cringe at the lyrics, and request that Jason Newsted sing them

live as part of a "Metallica medley" of their early metal tunes, the images of ravaging, deadly spectres straight out of the *Book of Revelations* is a quintessential heavy metal icon that suited the fledgling Metalli-heads to a tee.

Nevertheless, for all its heavy metal demons'n' wizards approach "The Four Horsemen" still has its moments, in particular the third verse, which introduces the deadly protagonists and what they bring: "Time: Has taken its toll on you/The lines that crack your face, Famine: Your body it has torn through/Withered in every place, Pestilence: For what you had to endure/And what you have put others through, Death: Deliverance for you for sure/There is nothing that you can do".

How much of this apocalyptic vision had, in fact, been brought about by James Hetfield's Christian Scientist upbringing? It's almost as if Hetfield is using the biblical totem for revenge and punishment as a terror weapon that he is unleashing back upon those holier-than-thou types who had surrounded him in childhood. It's almost as if Hetfield is saying, "it doesn't matter what you do or how you do it because the world is already fucked, and judgement is coming regardless of who or what you are."

Of course, it's way easier to believe that in the rush to record the song the band sat around and watched movies like *Conan The Barbarian* or *Excalibur* and among the cinematic thunder of hooves and clashing of steel swords Hetfield thought, "Hey, that's a very heavy metal thing to write about and we need some lyrics right now." Given the last verse about the gathering of warriors, the strapping on of armour and the swinging of hammers of judgement, the genesis of "The Four Horsemen" is far more likely to be of the latter than any deep-rooted swipe at a hypocritical society at large.

Motorbreath

Strangely the only solo Hetfield song on the album, "Motorbreath" is again one of the many life-affirming anthems that litter *Kill 'Em All*. Whether it's written in homage to Motörhead's own self-titled ode to an amphetamine-led life – with which the song clearly shares a musical lineage – is unclear, but whatever, "Motorbreath" kicks serious butt.

As Hetfield was a fan of dragster racing it's likely "Motorbreath" is written not only in tribute to his love for fast cars being driven at reckless speeds (something Dave Mustaine would repeat for "502" on Megadeth's 1987 *So Far So Good...So What!* album), but also to the unyielding, never-be-conquered state of mind that many a young, testosterone-pumped metal fan will adopt to survive in a world telling them to smarten up.

Being a metal fan in the early Eighties, with long hair and a denim or leather jacket sewn with patches, was much like being in any other subculture – a right to be earned, and once earned then defended. Parents, teachers, peer networks and the extended disapproving scowl of mainstream society in general can have many an effect on a young man. Some go off the rails in a fight against authority and acceptance, and end up in a life of spiralling crime. Most others simply learn to shut out the agendas of others who disapprove of their choices and concentrate on what gets them through living their lives – in this case, heavy metal. As Hetfield spits, "Motorbreath – It's how I live my life I can't do it any other way/I am taking down you know whatever is in my way" it should leave the listener in no doubt that this is again another song where metal is indeed the message.

Jump in the Fire

"Jump In The Fire" is just one song in a very long line of numbskull heavy metal tunes that stand in supposed devotion to the Horned One. Black Sabbath are inappropriately credited with having started the whole "We're in league with Satan" heavy metal-type lyrics from back in the early Seventies. It's inappropriate because the vast majority of bassist Geezer Butler's lyrics were in fact written as warnings against the dark powers of all manner of underworld denizens. The actual song "Black Sabbath" itself is the supposed last words of a man confronted by Satan on his day of judgement. Admittedly, "Lord Of This World", another Sabbath classic, perhaps does more to contribute to Satan's good PR inasmuch

as it speaks from a non-judgemental position. Yet the very fact that heavy metal bands, who were already ostracized from the mainstream musical community and derided by their more "accomplished" peers, dared to even write about Satan in such as fashion was enough for the Bible-bashers of the western world to leap into action. Suddenly Ozzy's crucifix chain was a sign of blasphemy rather than protection, and every metal band going was in league with the devil, from the kabuki-clad Kiss (Knights In Satan's Service according to some!) to even the hard-drinking boogie boys AC/DC.

By the time Ozzy's solo album landed in 1980 with the infamous "Mr Crowley" track – an ode to the so-called "evilest man who ever lived", part-time devil worshipper and full-time charlatan, Aleister Crowley – heavy metal had basically sold its soul to Satan wholesale in order to ride a wave of notoriety and reap the benefits of record sales.

With the advent of Venom came the next step – a celebration of all things dark and occult. Heavy metal, reasoned its protagonists anyway, was never meant to be universally liked – it was meant to scare and challenge, or, at the very least, annoy authority figures. With album titles such as *Black Metal* and *Welcome to Hell* and a theatrical image built on inverted crucifixes, pentagrams and black magic, Venom were the ultimate anti-authority figures. It also helped that they played twice as fast as Motörhead and just as loud.

Metallica were suckers for Venom. Lars in particular dug the speed at which the band managed to crank out their black metal anthems, while James found their OTT dark lyrics devilishly good fun.

Musically, "Jump In The Fire" is far removed from the high distortion of Venom, sounding akin to an old Accept riff, but lyrically, it was pure NWOBHM and could easily have come straight from the grooves of *Welcome To Hell*.

In "Jump In The Fire", the demon narrator is blatantly inviting the listener to join him in hell and dance in defiance. Again, the song is a rebel, fuck-authority anthem that proved wildly popular at Metallica's early shows. The infectiously catchy yet simple riff propels you forward, and as the drums crash along your head starts

Over page: the four horsemen – Cliff, Kirk, Lars and a mains-wired James Hetfield.

to bounce in sympathy. By the time Kirk's frantic lead break dances across the speakers you're in full-on air guitar/headbang interface mode. If nothing else "Jump In The Fire" proves that you don't have to be clever to write a first-class heavy metal anthem!

(Anesthesia) – Pulling Teeth

Being a bass guitar solo there are obviously no lyrics to discuss, but how can anyone re-appraise *Kill 'Em All* without mentioning the showpiece of the god-like genius on bass who was Cliff Burton? How many other debut records by a young heavy metal band have you come across that actually have the brass balls big enough to even include an instrumental, let alone one by a bassist, who, traditionally at least, must rank even lower than the drummer when it comes to solo spots? But Metallica weren't interested in playing along to convention. Sure, at this stage in their careers they wore their influences on their denim sleeves, that much was plain to see and hear, but that didn't mean that they harboured no ambitions to be perceived as being innovators themselves. Already, just by making *Kill 'Em All*, Metallica were standing alone in a field of one when it came to extreme US metal bands. Exodus, Slayer and Anthrax would soon all follow, but Metallica were streets ahead in terms of ambition. In fact, had the band had their way Cliff's solo and the Ulrich/Burton jam dubbed "Pulling Teeth" wouldn't have been the only "weird" bit on the record, as Metallica were well aware of the prodigious talent they harboured within the band. Part of the reason Cliff found Metallica so appealing was that he was allowed to play "lead bass" in the line-up, and he had many ideas to throw into the fire. However, *Kill 'Em All*'s producer, Paul Curico, and manager, Johnny Zazula, who let's not forget was fronting the cash for these recordings, were not having any of it. Legend has it that having indulged the band with the inclusion of the solo in the first instance (largely because the band didn't have a

tenth "proper" song ready anyway) the production duo simply weren't prepared to confuse the target audience any further. "Keep It Simple, Stupid" was the production motto, and Cliff would find himself being locked out of the recording booths so he physically couldn't record any more bass weirdness onto any of the tracks! As James would later recall: "Cliff had all kinds of shit that he wanted to record on his bass, and the producers would say, 'Well, it doesn't sound right.' Of course it didn't sound right! It wasn't fuckin' normal! But it's how we wanted to sound. Those guys were too fuckin' sterile. We were out there trying to create new sounds, and they were shootin' us down from the beginning" (3.49).

Whiplash

As heavy metal anthems go, the Hetfield/Ulrich-penned "Whiplash" has to rank in the premier division. Indeed, so integral to the Metallica ethos on life is the song that the band lifted a core lyric from it to use across the back cover – "bang the head that does not bang" – another clear, life-affirming statement from the very metal maestros of San Francisco. Over in Europe "Whiplash" was remixed (re-introducing the extended drum intro back into the middle of the song at louder volume) and issued as a limited-edition 12" picture disc by the new Music For Nations label, who had picked up the Metallica contract. Backed with supposedly "live" versions of "Phantom Lord" and "Seek and Destroy" (later it would emerge that actually they were "live in the rehearsal room" to save on costs) it was these three tunes that undoubtedly captured the adrenaline craziness and addictive qualities of Metallica.

Every band needs a rallying anthem, and though it might be argued that Metallica had an overflow of such romps through metal's clichéd graveyard, "Whiplash" still stands at the centre of *Kill 'Em All*'s formidable fury. It's almost as if each musician is challenging the other to outdo him as the song thrashes along at breakneck speed, and if there is any one song on the album graphically captured by the cover picture of the bloody sledgehammer, then "Whiplash" has to be it.

Everything about the song screams inane defiance

Kill 'em All

The Hammett/Hetfield twin-axe attack!

just for the sheer hell of it. Heavy metal isn't clever, it says, but it is damn big, and a whole lot of fun when it's played like this and you try to keep up with it.

From start to finish the song sounds like a whacked-out but spontaneous jam session captured live on tape, from the rolling double bass drum intro to the chopping guitars, and Kirk's wild solos right down to the gung-ho lyrics. And even if James Hetfield had actually thought about the lyrics for an aeon then he couldn't have done any better of a job than he did in the five minutes it took him to nail the utter physical abandonment of Metallica fans in mid-headbang – and then he would've almost certainly ruined the near-perfect stream of consciousness phrasing that the song demanded.

Lyrically, of course, the song could have (and probably was) inspired by one of the band's many stints in San Francisco at the Waldorf or Stone theatres, when Metallica began to realize that they had gained a grass roots support of local headbangers, mad for the band's adrenaline-fuelled guitars. Anyway, as every fan knows, you can't be taken seriously as a real metal band until you write your own self-referential anthem, just like Motörhead, Iron Maiden or, God bless 'em, Manowar.

Phantom Lord

The name of the song pre-dates Metallica by some way as it is also the name of James's first proper band, prior to that of even Leather Charm, and way before he even met Lars! Lyrically, the song belongs in the same Dungeons and Dragons ballpark as "The Four Horsemen" – all battle cries and leathered armies. The Phantom Lord himself sounds as if he is straight out of a Frank Frazetta fantasy painting mixed with a good dose of every Hollywood spook's favourite villain, Count Dracula, with his patented "hear the cry of war" line.

Like many a young lyricist Hetfield found himself limited by the actual song structure that his bandmates had written ("Phantom Lord" again being an Ulrich/Hetfield/Mustaine co-production). As their careers progressed and James grew more experienced,

like most other maturing songwriters he would go on to experiment with lyrical melodies first, and then the songs would be written around them afterwards, thereby capturing a more mature structure. But back in these early days James' instincts, like many others, was to cram whatever words seemed appropriate into the necessary space before the next riff came pummelling down or the next lead break seared across the speakers. It's hardly surprising, then, that the lyrics border on dark fantasy nonsense – after all, this is Metallica and lyrics about gambolling spring lambs somehow wouldn't fit the vibe. Equally then, nor is it a surprise that the lyrics rather clumsily rhyme in time with the music: "Hear the cry of war/Louder than before/With his sword in hand/To control the land."

No Remorse

Perhaps the most musically advanced of the *Kill 'Em All* tunes, "No Remorse" even hinted at the direction for which Metallica would eventually become renowned, with its distinct parts and rhythm changes. Even lyrically "No Remorse" picks upon a central "war is mad" theme that James would return to many times to come in

"For Whom The Bell Tolls", "Disposable Heroes", "Battery", and most poignantly, "One".

In this song, the narrator is seemingly caught up in an assault on the battlefield ("Soldiers are hounding/Bodies are mounting/Cannons are shouting to take their abuse") and yet surrounded by chaos, death and disorientation he still maintains at least some focus on the job at hand – killing the enemy. Given the fist-punching anthems of the album's previous songs, the reality-check of "No Remorse" stands out like a sore thumb. Gone are the fantasy creatures that prey on the weak of "The Four Horsemen" or "Phantom Lord" and in their place stands something far more terrible that every Metallica fan can place in the real world, the hellish and all too vividly familiar visage of war.

In fact, some of the later lines to "No Remorse" such as "Only the strong survive/No will to save the weaker race" are clearly unearthed once more in *Master of Puppets*' thunderous opener, "Battery", with its all-too-familiar, "Smashing all that cower/The weak are ripped and torn away" chorus lines. Upon closer inspection though, it seems that Hetfield has a very specific battle in mind, as he not only references guns and cannons but also swords. With the lack of any horses being mentioned we can rule out any direct thievery from Iron Maiden's classic Crimean war chant "The Trooper" with its "Bloody roar of the Russian guns", but it still leaves one wondering whether James had watched any particularly gripping WWI films or harrowing documentaries before he put pen to paper.

However, despite the noble sentiments it is tempting to read too much into these early lyrics, since the song could almost as easily be paying as much homage to the mythical idea that listening to metal music makes you strong and undefeatable as much as it is any meaningful anti-war epic. For that Metallica fans would have to wait another couple of albums.

An ironic (but feelgood) footnote is that come 1984, Motörhead – one of Metallica's seminal influences – took a lesson from one of their most popular students when Lemmy and co named their redemptive "Best-of" *No Remorse*. And like it was for Metallica before them "No Remorse" is as much a necessary state of mind as it is a song, an album or anything else.

Seek and Destroy

Every album deserves at least one song that its creators cannot kill off due to die-hard fan worship. Indeed, the day Metallica refuse to perform (at least in part) the familiar 10-note opening salvo of "Seek And Destroy" could very well be their last, as they will almost certainly be lynched by an angry mob decked out in *Kill 'Em All* shirts. If "Whiplash" is *Kill 'Em All*'s dark soul and "Hit The Lights" its primal driving force, then "Seek And Destroy" is undoubtedly its malevolent, predatory, beating heart.

Hugely influenced by the late Seventies cult classic film *The Warriors* (a film that later Metallica touring partners Twisted Sister would unofficially adopt as "theirs") "Seek And Destroy" broods with a simmering, barely contained sense of inevitable violence, much like Iron Maiden's masterful '81 classic "Killers".

Quite what the original crime that has been inflicted upon the narrator to cause the hunt is never explained, and as it unfolds, "Seek and Destroy" paints a picture of the urban pressure cooker jammed full to the brim with the disillusioned and disenfranchised young thugs who make up Anthony Burgess's nightmare future vision of society in *A Clockwork Orange*, the novel in which teenagers kill for thrills and kicks.

That said, lines like: "There's an evil feeling in our brains/But it's nothing new/You know it drives us insane" are straight out of the gonzoid black lyric book of The Misfits' Glenn Danzig. "We are 138", "Teenagers From Mars" and the immortal "Mommy, Can I Go Out And Kill Tonight?" are but three Misfits classics that, lyrically at least, "Seek And Destroy" could very easily be traced back to.

Musically though, the sinister intro riff and the middle breakdown with its almost deliberate cues to the crowds to mosh is, structurally at least, almost identical to Diamond Head's "Dead Reckoning". No one said you had to be original when writing a great song – just pick a great song and improve it.

Big and Clever: The Band relax while on tour.

Metal Militia

As album closers go, "Metal Militia" hardly goes out with any added "bang" value, though it does rather cheesily feature the only overdubbed special effect sound (presumably to justify the producer's fee) in the form of the marching boots as the track fades out over Hetfield's closing shriek.

When it comes to dumb lyrics, "Metal Militia" must ultimately take a bow. Quite what points Hetfield is trying to convey to the listener are lost in a mire of the silliest metal words the band had penned thus far. It's back to fantasy land, with dark armies of the night and creepy, all powerful demons threatening to rape and pillage your families and lands. The song even includes the immortal line "What will befall you/The metalization of your inner soul?"

It's tempting to say that *Kill 'Em All* must be the only album in US sales history to achieve platinum status (one million-plus sales) with a line such as this, but then when one considers that *Quiet Riot* went multi-platinum and those gods of the cornball lyric Kiss regularly shit platinum discs every time they release an album, the mystery dissipates. People obviously don't give a damn what the words are about if the music is good enough, and many a lyric is simply turned into a suitably mindless chant that seems to fit the mood of the song.

There is nothing wrong at all with the use of fantasy lyrics in metal songs – Rainbow's Ronnie James Dio and thousands of European heavy metal bands have made long careers warbling about dragons and rainbows, but by the time the band would come to record such fantasy songs like "Enter Sandman" or "Of Wolf And Man" from '91's *Metallica* opus, the balance between fantasy and the ridiculous had been mastered.

Tellingly, from this point on after "Metal Militia" any demons of the night that Metallica were to write about would be of the far more sinister, occult types conjured up from the diseased mind of HP Lovecraft rather than the garbled fumblings of a frustrated Dungeons and Dragons gamesmaster.

3

Ride the Lightning

Behind the scenes

Martin: "Gradually, though, the scene changed – we were aware of what was happening on the underground, that people were taping *Kill 'Em All* and passing it along, and we could see over that first 12 months the sales going up steadily and continually. It went up from five hundred to a thousand to three thousand copies a week. By the time *Ride the Lightning* came out, they were just ready to explode.

"I remember that Shades in London was the big metal record shop at the time, and the week of release on *Ride...* they had 1,500 copies of the album already in bags with receipts on the morning it came out, because they knew what the demand was going to be like. I went down there and there was a queue for the record stretching right the way through the heart of Soho. Funny thing was, the national charts realized *Ride...* was going to go in and because they hadn't heard of the band they rang up Shades as an independent non-chart specialist to ask them how many copies they had sold. Shades told 'em it was 1,500 copies and counting, and it stunned them to silence!"

"By the time *Ride...* came out we were actually in charge of the band financially, as Johnny Z had run out of money. We put up all the cash to keep them going. MFN brought the band over to record *Ride...* in Denmark in Sweet Silence studios. I thought at the time that it was the right thing to do – to get them out of San Francisco and away from the hangers-on, and get them to concentrate on making the next record, y'know. How wrong was I? Turns out that Sweet Silence was just far enough away from London to deter me from flying in regularly to check up on them, and it was also far enough away from Copenhagen to deter them from going into town, but the bloody studios had its own bar serving Elephant Beer! They used up the budget we'd set in five weeks! I'd ring Lars up and ask how it was going and he'd be like, 'Don't worry Martin, it's sounding great', but after five weeks and not hearing anything I decided to fly in to check on what they had actually done. Turns out they'd just about got the bloody drum sound sorted. After that, thankfully, they knuckled down and, hey, they wrote *Ride the Lightning*, so I can't complain. It went gold in the UK (100K) which in turn took *Kill 'Em All* over the gold mark too. In fact, by the time Metallica were picked up for a major label, in the UK they'd already got three gold records behind them because *...Puppets* did that in a matter of weeks!"

How long were Metallica out on tour for *Ride the Lightning*?

Martin: "I think we had them out for nearly 12 months, but they were writing *...Puppets* while they were touring. I think we put something like £100K into them to keep the band going during that period. Mind you, we made about ten times that back out of the record! You can't tour like that these days because it's so much more expensive."

Gem: "You used to be able to get a band, their back-line and a three-man crew in a transit across Europe, but these days bands just don't want to put that sort of work in."

Martin: "American bands do work harder than their English counterparts – it's true. They will press the flesh every day, do interviews 24 hours a day and play a gig every day of the year if you let them. British bands start cracking up after three months of touring America or once they've recorded the album sit back and think that their bit is done and they're gonna be on *Top of the Pops*!"

Did you expect *Ride...* to sound like it did?

Martin: "I wasn't all that surprised, actually. I really believed in the band from the get-go and after *Kill 'Em All* that band played hundreds and hundreds of shows to get their craft right. I knew that they'd all been working on new material and I figured that James and Lars had a few ideas tucked away. It's a remarkable metal record, no question."

Ride the Lightning (1984)

'The main difference between *Kill 'Em All* and *Ride the Lightning* was that we had Cliff and Kirk, who brought a diversity and musical edge to the whole thing. We wanted to try to do some different things, not to play "Whiplash" all the time, which we knew would get boring. We were really proud of the way *Ride the Lightning* came out. We were really thrilled with the sound.'

Lars Ulrich, 1992 (1.26)

Ride the Lightning was the start of the professional Metallica. Now no longer just the James and Lars show, the band had four equally contributing members who were each out to push the others to their musical limits.

Even a casual comparative listen between the first and second Metallica records would beg the question – is this even the same band? Of course that early signature Hetfield shriek and stabbing rhythm sound is still apparent, as are Kirk Hammett's fluid solos, but it

was all change for everything else. The sheer scale of the songwriting on *Ride...* is nothing less than an ocean apart from its primitive predecessor. From the unexpected lilting acoustic intro of "Fight Fire With Fire" through the spiralling chords of the title track, to the epic swirls of live mainstay "For Whom The Bell Tolls" and the 'dark ballad', "Fade To Black", *Ride...* is every inch a classic record. And we haven't even mentioned "Trapped Under Ice" or the small matter of "Creeping Death"...

Businesswise too, Metallica were also taking huge steps. Though they started the recording of *Ride...* in early '84 at Sweet Silence studios in Denmark, at the behest of their new European label Music For Nations

Kirk's Renaissance Man jokes soon wore thin.

Ride the Lightning

Metallica step onto the big stages as Ride the Lightning takes off across Europe.

(largely because manager Johnny Zazula had run out of cash now he was also representing Anthrax and Exciter, much to Metallica's irritation), the band would end the *Ride...* touring cycle in a major label deal with the powerful Elektra Records, but also with a new, and equally heavyweight management team, QPrime, who handled business affairs for the huge-selling Def Leppard.

With a genuine metal classic in the can, two new pro-active record labels battling their cause in the two main markets and a powerful management organization, Metallica were finally on their way.

Fight Fire with Fire

An acoustic guitar? On a Metallica song? You can almost still hear the shocked groans of the original Metalli-fans when *Ride*'s... opening chords tuned out not to be a battery of charging guitars but the false security of Hetfield's gently strumming acoustic guitar. Of course it isn't long before those familiar, if now crunchier, Hetfield riffs come crashing down and the song takes on a punkier, traditionally more Metallica-ish feel.

The acoustic intro is set up to convey the idyllic

METALLICA50

setting of the perfect day with its blue skies, shining sun on a bright, fresh spring morning – the last Earth will see before nuclear armageddon!

Written at the nervous height of the Cold War when the hawkish Reagan administration had just revealed plans for the so-called "Star Wars" defence program (a space-based laser-and-nuclear-armed satellite "defence system" designed to protect mainland US), the song captures a paranoid state of mind that a lot of Americans were fearful of.

Nuclear armageddon, massive destruction and the horrors of post-nuclear mutation are prime lyrical fodder for metal songwriters, since the images of fantastic-sized explosions and twisted deaths fit perfectly with the über-aggressive thrashings of extreme metal bands such as Metallica.

However, once again, it is pertinent to ask whether James Hetfield is deliberately taking an anti-war stance, as he might have done earlier on "No Remorse". At the time, every home in California had rather famously been delivered an information pamphlet detailing what citizens could and should do in the event of a nuclear attack by the dreaded Soviet "Red Menace". This was the same pamphlet that spurred Dave Mustaine to name his post-Metallica band Megadeth, no less. Lines like, "Soon to fill our lungs the hot winds of death/The gods are laughing so take your last breath", are clearly the result of someone watching too many documentaries about nuclear survival than is actually healthy.

However, for the very first time there is another more complex theme emerging in "Fight..." that would also appear throughout a variety of later Metallica songs, and that is the "us versus them" scenario. The "us" in this situation is the common man – the Metallica fan being addressed – and, therefore by default, one must suspect that the "them" is "The Man" – the government, or the establishment – those faceless politicians and civil servants who govern our daily lives, and who are perceived to lack accountability.

"Fight Fire With Fire" opens with the line "Do unto others as they have done to you/But what the hell is this world coming to?", a pastiche on biblical phrasing and

The secret mutations of rock stars pt 27: Kirk Hammett's penis hand.

lecture for sure, but also the beginning cries of the dis-empowered common man. And, as we will see, it is a theme to which Hetfield would return many more times, particularly on "Escape" and later the whole of the *...And Justice For All* album.

Ride the Lightning

There is certainly no debate to be had on what this particular song is about, given that the album's front cover depicts an empty electric chair powered by lightning! "Ride..." is one of the first songs that Cliff Burton had an active writing hand in when he joined Metallica in early '83, and the track still features Dave Mustaine's original opening riffs. The track's sweeping chords and classy time changes have Burton's influence all over them, and it's clear that the talented bassist added a hitherto unseen maturity to the Metallica songwriting structure that was allowing the band to explore new areas with growing confidence.

Whether or not Metallica are choosing to take a stand on the death penalty issue here is debatable. Again, it's more likely that James considered the exploration of the last thoughts of a condemned man strapped to an electric chair to be perfect subject matter for the song's chopping melodies and stabbing solos. You can be sure that in a similar lyrical circumstance U2 would've rattled on about human rights – Bono would be clad in chains, shaved of head and wistfully reminiscing over his missing family in a "see, I'm human too" kind of way, while at the opposite end of the spectrum, Slayer would've written it up as "Fry You Fucker!" Metallica chose to explore the first-person scenario and leave the morality issues out of the equation.

If you are a cheap thrill-seeker or an avid fan of horror novels in all their gory glory then *Ride...* is for you. Equally though, if you are a person of deep conviction and firmly anti-death penalty, then intense lines like, "Who made you God to say/'I'll take your life from

Keeping it real back in the clubs.

you!'" and "Sweat chilling cold/As I watch death unfold/Consciousness my only friend" are likely to raise the blood pressure and rage at the inhumanity and hypocrisy of such a system. Tellingly, one of Hetfield's own lyrical heroes, Nick Cave, chose the same non-judgemental, first-person perspective when he wrote his universally acclaimed classic "The Mercy Seat" in 1988.

Fittingly, we also once again have to ask the question is the "you" in the "Who made you God?" line, the "you" the condemned man challenges from the chair, the faceless aspect of a totalitarian government sending an innocent man or a political prisoner to his death? Is this another case of Hetfield exploring his "us versus them" thinking?

For Whom the Bell Tolls

Another grunt's song? Like "No Remorse" and "Disposable Heroes" after it, "...Tolls" tells the story of a foot soldier ordered into the chaos of battle and expected to lay down his life for an obscure military objective. But there the similarities end to anything that has gone before. For in lyrical terms "...Tolls" is a league above its stunted predecessor, and this writer at least would argue that it even has the edge on its much-loved successor on *Master of Puppets*. Indeed, the sense of innocence harnessed within these lyrics are put across so eloquently that it wouldn't even be out of place alongside a collection of Wilfred Owen or Siegfried Sassoon WWI poetry. You want evidence for this outrageous statement? – look no further than the lines: "Take a look to the sky just before you die/It's the last time he will/Blackened roar, massive roar fills the crumbling sky/Shattered goal fills his soul with a ruthless cry". These lines are almost style-perfect war poetry, wherein the writer brings the reader into the hellish vision of war by addressing them directly in their world of the normal before confronting them with the brutal realities of conflict. The colourful semantic-laden adjectives that

James uses throughout the song help paint a vivid picture of the chaos surrounding the soldier – the "shouting" guns, the "blackened" roar and the "shattered" goals – and he does this while also capturing the confusion and general numbness of the soldier in the story – "A stranger now are his eyes to this mystery/He hears the silence so loud".

Any number of war movies could have acted as the inspiration for this particular song but it is important to note that "...Tolls" predated the plethora of revisionist Vietnam war movies that graced cinemas in the mid-Eighties, such as *Platoon*, *Full Metal Jacket* and perhaps the song's closest cinematic cousin, *Hamburger Hill*.

Given that James would again return to the subject of war on many more occasions after the completion of "For Whom The Bell Tolls", it is obviously a subject that he not only thinks befitting of the musical dynamic of Metallica, but also a subject that interests him greatly.

Fade to Black

Without doubt the lyrical heart of *Ride the Lightning*, "Fade To Black" is also the finest set of lyrics that Hetfield had yet penned. As it follows "For Whom The Bell Tolls" rather aptly, so does the lyrical maturity. In this song we bear witness to the narrator writing their suicide note and gently saying goodbye to the world they no longer wish to be part of.

It is tribute to the increasing maturing of the Metallica camp that they felt confident enough to even tackle such a thorny and complex subject as suicide, let alone that they more than surpassed such lyrics with such evocative and restrained music. For there is no mistaking it, "Fade To Black" is a ballad. Sure, it is a remorseful, melancholy-seeped song and certainly a world apart from the drippy, AOR "power" ballads that would hog the Eighties rock charts, but its still a ballad by any other name.

There is little doubt that Hetfield had been stretching his powers of articulation to breaking point in the search to be different to all the other metal thrashing mad types who were now chasing down the coat-tails of his band and who, like Metallica only a year previous, were content to dwell solely on matters that were either heavy or metal. But it is songs such as "Fade To Black" that elevated Metallica straight out of the so-called thrash pack. For anyone to diminish or relegate Metallica to a position of mere "thrashers" once they had completed works such as "Fade…" or "…Tolls" would be nothing short of utter ignorance. Could a mindless thrash band handle the haunting phrasings of "Fade To Black"'s last, almost delicate lines?

Bizarrely, but perhaps not unexpectedly, "Fade To Black" was one of the new songs that the band were very nervous about recording, after an earlier decision to pre-release four *Ride…* songs on a demo tape to the die-hards resulted in a backlash from unhappy metal heads. Once past the hostile refrains of "Fight Fire With Fire" (minus the acoustic intro, natch) the fans were puzzled by tracks such as "Ride the Lightning", "Creeping Death" and utterly defeated by the extended instrumental "When Hell Freezes Over" (later changed to the more familiar 'Call of Ktulu'). The changing rhythms and extended, naturally slower instrumental workouts came at the expense of speed, speed and more speed. As early adopters of the Metallica cause and fierce defenders of the metal faith these die-hards reacted angrily to Metallica's so-called "development". As a close follower of such underground networks Lars in particular was affected by the backlash, but soon worry turned to irritation and then hardened resolve as Metallica stood by the quality of the music that they knew they were creating. Much to their eternal credit, Metallica refused to compromise or be held to ransom by what turned out to be a passionately vocal but still tiny minority of those who would eventually own the album.

As Lars would later attest: "I can't help but worry about what other people think (of new material), but I shouldn't worry, because I feel like we're playing for ourselves, and if we wanna do a ballad, or whatever, we'll

do a ballad. If people don't like it, fuck 'em!" (3.56)

Just think – some of the earliest Metallica fans would've robbed the rest of us of "Fade To Black"!

Trapped Under Ice

Back to the first person we go in an impending death scenario. Like "Fight Fire With Fire" and many *Kill 'Em All*-era songs it seems that the music to "Trapped Under Ice" was written way before the lyrics ever came to fruition. The short, stilted verses are written to match the ferocity of the song's central, slicing riff. This song, like "Escape" which follows, is an Ulrich/Hetfield/Hammett co-composition, and it's tempting to say that the others missed the experimental hand of Cliff Burton! Yet it's testament to exactly how far Metallica had developed as a song writing unit (even though they were still only 20–21 years old!) that compared to the youthful thrashings of any of the *Kill 'Em All* material, "Trapped…" is a relative masterpiece.

Much like "Ride the Lightning" itself, "Trapped Under Ice" dwells upon the last thoughts of a man being slowly frozen alive by cryogenics. As the song progresses he can feel the ice slowly creeping up his veins and rendering him into a "cryonic state". Another classic nightmare tale made real for the purposes of matching the dramatic effect of the music "Trapped…" is hardly a lyrical masterpiece to rank alongside "Fade…" or "…Tolls", but nevertheless it does its job effectively

The song was also the very last one written before the band were bundled into Sweet Silence studios, and though it is tempting to suggest that this last-minute rushing forced the pace and clearly affected the quality of the lyrics and the song in general, it's probably not a bit of it true, as that same last-minute creative burst also yielded "Escape" and "For Whom The Bell Tolls"!

The live appearances continued as Ride the Lightning*'s popularity grew. Lars was obviously pleased.*

Escape

Perhaps the best early example of James Hetfield's refusal to accept the status quo, "Escape" seems to be as much about a freeing of the mind to recognize the implicit connections between authority and repression on a social level as it is any physical escape of an individual from a prison cell per se. "Escape" neatly picks up the threads that "Ride…" and "Fight Fire With Fire" had laid down before it.

With an uncharacteristically commercial bent to the melody behind the vocals it is James's singing on "Escape" and "Fade to Black" that most likely convinced him that he could become a world-class metal vocalist.

Legend has it that prior to the recording of these songs James suffered from an acute lack of confidence over his vocal talent and he cited Iron Maiden's Bruce Dickinson and Judas Priest's Rob Halford as being what

he saw as definitive heavy metal singers. Talented as both Halford and Dickinson are, neither one could handle the brutish snarl that many a Metallica classic requires, and certainly neither could deliver a vocal line while playing the complex rhythms that Hetfield lays down on every song! Nevertheless, so overwhelming were Hetfield's fears of being unable to keep up the performance night after night on tour that the band agreed to approach Armoured Saint's more classic metal-voiced singer John Bush, who was also managed by Q-Prime. Bush turned Metallica down, preferring to concentrate on his own band instead, though in a bizarre twist of fate he would later quit the Saint to join long-time Metallica friends Anthrax as a replacement for Joey Belladonna.

Lyrically then, "Escape" is a powerful affirmation of the individual's right in the face of restricting, overbearing state control. From the outset Hetfield is on the warpath, ridiculing the wrongdoing that has been inflicted upon the narrator – "Can't get caught in the

Creeping Death

endless circle/Ring of stupidity" before the chorus settles upon the central theme – the right to be free – "One with my mind, they just can't see/No need to hear things that they say/Life is my own to live my own way".

The lyrics are distinctly Orwellian, and it would be no surprise to learn that James Hetfield is a fan of George Orwell's totalitarian nightmare saga *1984*, or Aldous Huxley's *Brave New World*.

One line in particular gives a key indication as to where Hetfield is coming from – "Feed my brain with your so-called standards/Who says that I ain't right?" Once more it's the voice of the little man standing up for his rights. Is it too much of a leap of faith to suggest that Hetfield was reacting against the increasing political power and voice of right-wing organizations such as the PMRC (the Parents Music Resource Center), who were becoming increasingly vocal in their condemnations of more high-profile metal acts such Iron Maiden and Ozzy Osbourne? Maybe James was taking their viewpoint to its logical state-controlled conclusion as if to tell them – it won't matter if you get your way, because when I close my eyes I'm still me and I still think the way I choose so you won't beat me. Of course, Orwell's *1984* had the nefarious "Thought Police" to counter any such freedom of mental expression...

You can say what you want and wax lyrical about many an exceptionally written lyric, but in the end sometimes it simply doesn't matter what you write if the music behind it is just as stunning. 'Creeping Death' is that song on *Ride the Lightning*.

Rather strangely, this tale of murder most foul is set in ancient Egypt, maybe James had been watching one too many re-runs of Charlton Heston in *The Ten Commandments* before entering the studio? Rather cleverly though, the narrator's voice changes as the dynamic of the song moves through its various phases.

The initial verse sets the scene: that Pharaoh has been an unjust ruler, that the Hebrews of Goshen are rising up in rebellion and that they have sent an assassin in their name to strike revenge upon Pharaoh's son. The chorus powers along in mock-biblical script with its "So let it be written/So let it be done" coupling used to great dramatic effect.

Verse two is pure Old Testament revenge and retribution as we hear of bushes of fire, blood in the Nile, plagues and eternal darkness. Then the second chorus chimes in again, building into what is, for many, the highpoint of any Metallica gig when thousands of fist-pumping hands are held aloft and throats scream, "DIE! DIE! DIE!", as Hetfield continues his lurching vocal line, "...As I creep across the land". It's pure heavy metal theatre and nothing short of orchestrated genius on the part of Metallica, who clearly conceived of the audience participation when writing this mid-song breakdown. Every band needs an anthem to hold up tired fans, especially when the set consists of several epic work-outs, and in "Creeping Death" Metallica certainly nailed theirs.

The final verse, then, is the voice of the gleeful but righteous assassin – "the destroyer" as he terms himself – as he homes in on his infant prey, creeping up the stairs and past the "Lamb's blood-painted door".

An awesome piece of live theatre and definitely a fine

example of when less is more, it's no wonder that nearly twenty years after its release "Creeping Death" remains one of the most popular tunes that Metallica have ever written.

Call of Ktulu

There isn't much to explain about "Ktulu", lyrically speaking anyway, as it is the second instrumental Metallica recorded. Though credited to a collective Hetfield/Ulrich/Burton/Mustaine line-up, one should be in no doubt that, given the "lead bass" credit in the sleeve notes and the name of the actual song itself, this was another Cliff Burton-led project. Burton, unlike the others, was a huge fan of the 1920s horror writer HP Lovecraft, but soon after his assimilation into the Metallica ranks his infectious enthusiasm for all things Lovecraftian and occult-based spread to the rest of the band, who considered the stories of insane ancient gods lurking in parallel dimensions to be majorly appropriate for an up-and-coming metal band to be interested in.

Howard Philips Lovecraft wrote many tales about the "unspeakable horrors" that lurked in the shadows, waiting for overly inquisitive humans to stumble upon, and he published most in his pulp magazine, *Weird Tales* from his New England retreat.

Many of Lovecraft's warped tales involve vengeful visitors from outer space, spiteful ancient gods returning to claim their birthright or the Promethian access of forbidden knowledge (usually retrieved from Miskatonic University, a pre-*Buffy*-style madhouse/school for paranormal researchers, but with bigger, nastier demons).

Several of Lovecraft's tales have been turned into low-budget horror flicks including *Re-Animator*, *From Beyond* and, more recently, *Dagon*.

Anybody wondering just what inspired Cliff when he recorded those way-out and very weird bass effects for "Ktulu", and later on "The Thing That Should Not Be" and "Orion", would do well to pick up one of Lovecraft's strange books and therein find the key.

4
Master of Puppets

'We're very much into using changes of mood and are trying to broaden out our musical base…We allowed ourselves considerable breathing space and opportunity to go in any direction we chose.'

Lars Ulrich, 1986 (1.26)

'I think lyrically, …*Puppets* is one of my favourite albums…'

James Hetfield, 1992 (1.27)

For many, the definitive album that Metallica have recorded is not the massive-selling self-titled album of 1991, but its 1986 predecessor, *Master of Puppets*. Certainly, in Europe …*Puppets* is still celebrated in much greater fashion than either …*And Justice For All* or *Metallica*, and it regularly turns up in music critics' top-albums-of-all-time polls, way ahead of its multi-million-selling cousins.

In three short years Metallica had made giant, genre-defying leaps in terms of songwriting depth and complexity. From "Seek and Destroy" to "The Thing That Should Not Be", from "Phantom Lord" to "Disposable Heroes" or "Jump In The Fire" to "Leper Messiah" – there simply is no comparison. *Ride the Lightning*'s classic

"For Whom The Bell Tolls" and "Fade To Black" have a hard time matching the powerful subtlety of "(Welcome Home) Sanitarium" or the dynamic rush of the …*Puppets* title track. Even the youthful aggression of *Kill 'Em All*'s "Motorbreath" or the more structured aggression of *Ride*'s… "Fight Fire With Fire" seem virtually muted when held up in comparison to the venomous rage unleashed by the album's bookend tracks, "Battery" and "Damage Inc".

On …*Puppets*, the extended musical work-outs that Metallica had hinted at on *Ride the Lightning*, "Fade To Black" and "Call of Ktulu" were now fully fleshed-out epics to be slowly digested rather than greedily consumed. It was – and remains – Metallica's finest hour.

Battery

Erroneously often believed to be another one of Hetfield's tortured soldier tales due to the title and the chopping, "battering" central riff, which is akin to the sound of artillery fire, "Battery" is the tale of a man gone mad.

It's likely that an idea to update the usual "metal is the message" ethos of the early songs took a different turn during "Battery"'s expression of strength. On the surface it seems as it the song is a life-affirming scream of defiance from someone refusing to submit to outside forces. But as it progresses it becomes clear that the song's narrator is without reason, and in the throes of a blood lust – "Hungry violence seeker feeding off the weaker/Breeding on insanity".

By this second verse we can no longer confuse lines such as "Lunacy has found me/Cannot kill the battery", as being anything military-based at all – this is about someone losing the plot and heading out on an unstoppable killing rampage.

Understanding this is also key in getting to grips with why there is a gentle Spanish strumming of the song (and album's intro) and its significance in terms of the larger theme of the whole album.

Yes, of course, the acoustic strumming is partly another teasing tactic, the same as Metallica employed with great effect on "Fight Fire With Fire", but instead of this being a picture of the perfect earth prior to nuclear devastation, this intro is a deeply personal moment, for it is the tranquillity of someone's mind which is about to be destroyed by murderous insanity.

Metallica had simply grown beyond the 'world is gonna' die horror subtexts of their earlier thrashier numbers and, at long last, managed to marry the lyrical potency of "Fade to Black" and "For Whom The Bell Tolls" to their furiously paced aggression.

If the *Ride the Lightning* album had a loose theme concerned with dying and death in general (which, let's face it, it did) then the theme connecting all the songs of *...Puppets* has to be about manipulation and betrayal. The betrayal might be of oneself by one's own mind as in "Battery", "Sanitarium" or the title song, or it could be manipulation by others who play on the fears of the

individual on such tracks as "Leper Messiah", "Disposable Heroes" and, to a lesser extent, perhaps even "Damage Inc" too.

One other observation of note to be made is the conceptual similarities between "Battery" and Megadeth's "Black Friday" from 1986's *Peace Sells...But Who's Buying?*. Both songs are about normal everyday Joes who suddenly snap and take up killing sprees for no apparent reason. Given the pride at stake, it's highly unlikely that either James or Dave Mustaine would consciously copy each other, but if nothing else it serves to show just how similar the two front men still remained in terms of the things that influenced them to write (but thinking about it, what about "Escape" and the sentiments behind the "Peace Sells" song as well? Hmmm...).

T-shirt Homage: James pays respect to The Misfits.

Master of Puppets

Hot in Here: Post-gig Metallica.

Metallica had never written an anti-drugs song before and it's unclear what made James tackle the subject at this point. Certainly, there has never been any evidence that any member of the band has ever developed any serious drug addiction (aside from the regular backstage party antics, that is), and James's much later alcohol rehab stint in 2000. However, as a touring rock band it's also inevitable that they had come across many an individual who had developed heroin or cocaine habits – not least of whom was Dave Mustaine, who for a time in the late Eighties, had considerable trouble in policing his narcotics intake.

The song "Master of Puppets" is not only a masterful exercise in observing an addict's behaviour, it's also a stroke of inspired genius as it turns the typical junkie state of mind song on its head to speak from the point of view of the drug itself. In this way the manipulation and betrayal aspects that were discussed earlier become far more potent in their delivery. The drug now has a personality and a mission – to fuck you up. The song strips the junkie of any power, he is simply a victim tossed around by the whims of the drug, his "master".

Indeed, the only use of the junkie's "voice" comes in the third stanza, after the eerie mid-song breakdown, where the painful cries of "master" echo down to silence before the start of the second act, heralded by the sound of James's crunching guitar grinding back with serious intent.

Now we hear the junkie howling with outrage that the dreams and the escape he has sought has turned out to be "lies" and he is left facing a world that treats him with contempt for being foolish enough to seek solace in heroin. The drug voice then hits back by revealing its true vocation – to rule and destroy the user completely – "I will occupy/I will help you die/I will run through you/Now I rule you too".

He might not have known at the time he came up with the two narrative voices that dominate the song, but James couldn't have written a more perfect moral tragedy in a classic style had he tried. There no good versus evil morality going on here, though: it's stupidity versus exploitation, victim versus user, hunter and prey.

The Thing That Should Not Be

The most surprising aspect of "…Thing" is that Cliff Burton doesn't even receive a hint of a song credit! The original HP Lovecraft fan in the band and the man who campaigned hard to record "Call of Ktulu" last time around, it was in fact James and Lars who came up with the concept for "Thing" and James who provided all the lyrics after reading Lovecraft's *Dagon* book.

In *Dagon* a young group of wealthy travellers are sailing off an island in the Mediterranean when a mysterious storm envelopes their boat, causing two to die and two others to flee to land. The survivors, now separated, attempt to summon help from the locals but

as they spend more time in the town they realize that all the locals are half-human/half-fish hybrids. The local priest had sold his soul and those of the townsfolk to an ancient underwater god, who returns to claim his sacrifices often and to bless his mutated "children" (imagine *The Wicker Man* meets *Waterworld* and you're only missing the gore and squid heads).

The townsfolk of Dagon crave nothing more than to return to the depths of the ocean and be at one with their master and god. From that point on it's cue the many gory deaths and some pretty horrible inter-species sex as well, in this twisted but chillingly good fun old tale.

James obviously liked the story too, as he remains faithful to the central plot throughout the song, referencing the "hybrid children" watching the sea and praying for their "father" to be set free underwater. The big nasty is referred to in pure Lovecraftian half-shadow as "the thing that should not be" and the "great old one"

that will "drain you of your sanity" and leave you dwelling in madness. Hetfield even paraphrases one of Lovecraft's most quoted lines, too – "Stranger eons (even) death may die" – which, coincidentally, had made its way on to the cover artwork of Iron Maiden's classic *Live After Death* a year previously.

"The Thing That Should Not Be" is a true work of art. Musically it was by far the most ambitious song Metallica had yet constructed, with Burton's basslines downtuned to almost bowel-shaking levels and Hammett's delectably deranged solos providing the perfect flourishes to James's eerie singing voice. What a far cry from the "Phantom Lord" of 1983 to the menacing delirium of "The Thing That should Not Be", crowed Metallica. And who could argue?

The song is also Metallica at their most experimental – not once since the recording of this song have they ever threatened to challenge themselves in such a manner again. Indeed, why should they – the point was made to perfection back in 1986!

Welcome Home (Sanitarium)

If "Fade To Black" was the heart of Ride the Lightning, then the centre of *...Puppets'* wounded soul has to be the deranged nightmare that is "Sanitarium". Inspired by Ken Kesey's novel *One Flew Over The Cuckoo's Nest*, which starred Jack Nicholson in the more famous film of the same name, "Sanitarium" is a genuine classic.

Those critics who argue that metal bands know nothing of the art of subtlety in songwriting have obviously never heard the intro chimes and Kirk's distant solo at the onset of "Sanitarium". That's their loss.

The song's narrator is the inmate in a facility who still retains the wherewithal to question whether he should lawfully be there. Like "Escape" before it there is certainly the suggestion that the prisoner has no actual reason to be confined and sees the treatment as manipulation ("Whisper things into my brain/Assuring me that I'm insane"). He is cynically confined and becoming institutionalized by the day ("Build my fear of what's out there/Cannot breathe the open air"). Like the character in "Escape", Sanitarium's narrator is reaching into his own mind to find release but this time within his dreams, where he sees "no locked doors or windows barred".

The character's confinement is causing his violent impulses in a vicious circle, but far from being insane he is able to articulate this – "They keep me locked up in this cage/Can't they see it's why my brain says rage?" This rage spills over in the last verse, where the cycle of anger/medication/anger is being dramatically illustrated by the ascending flurry of guitars and Lars' quickening drum beats, which were written to mirror the agitated state of the narrator when he finally flips out: "Mirror stares back hard/Kill – it's such a friendly word/Seems the only way/For reaching out again".

It is remarkable that in three short years Metallica had made the leap from writing about kicking ass and metal militias to their being able to illustrate with ease, and with deep complexity, the real-life horrors of the world at large.

It's relatively easy to wax lyrical and rant about nuclear horrors when you're using a guitar turned up to 11 and are able to make a noise akin to a bomb going off, and everyone will easily understand the limited point you are making. But it's far harder to actually hold on to people's attention once you have it, because you had better have something worthwhile to say if you're going to shout as loud as Metallica. Metallica's maturity and increasing skill in being able to address broader topics such as mental illness and imprisonment placed them on a higher, more accessible platform overnight as they now quite rightly had to be taken seriously as credible artists and performers. Critics who had previously dismissed Metallica as thrashy noise now had to eat their words and face up to their mistakes – because the ungainly and very noisy Metallica were suddenly all grown-up.

James and Kirk make beautiful music together.

Disposable Heroes

The most direct of the manipulation-themed songs on the album, "Disposable Heroes" is another of James's war stories, and with the exception of "One", it has to be the strongest. Indeed, the cover art for the album is directly connected to this particular song: the hands holding the puppet strings are connected to infinitesimal rows of white crosses representing the unnamed dead young soldiers of an equally nameless war.

Again, as with the title track, James also chose to dramatize the song from two separate viewpoints – one of the bewildered soldier fresh from the battlefield and the other, the harsh, unforgiving bark of a faceless general. "Disposable Heroes" must also rank as being the longest lyric that James had ever written by this point in his career too, as he takes his characters through a variety of scenarios.

The song's central character, a young soldier, has apparently spent his early life being brought up in a military academy – the line, "Life planned out before my birth, nothing could I say" backs this up. Others have ventured that it's possible James is offering us yet another one of his futuristic totalitarian military states, in which insane generals embark upon meaningless wars for war's sake. Whatever the year in which it's based, the soldier clearly sees himself as nothing more than a pawn, describing himself as a "victim of what said should be", i.e. at some point in his life someone else decided that he would be a soldier rather than him being allowed to choose, a point backed up by the line, "Servant 'til I fall".

The general's voice adopts an almost robot-like viewpoint as he casts a judgemental eye over the shellshocked young soldier while he hands him back to his family, claiming that he was "made of clay", that he was little more than an "empty shell". It could just as

The tours get bigger, the fanbase grows and the live shows grow. James wows the crowd…

Practice makes Perfect: Lars Ulrich keeps keeps it up on the drums at every opportunity!

easily have been a battlefield scene from a WWI movie in which a dismissive general passes comment over one shattered body before passing on to the next. Yet the cold, robot-like way the Army hands the son back to his family is striking: "21 only son/But he served us well/Bred to kill/Not to care/Do just as we say/Finished here, greetings death/He's yours to take away".

The scene is reminiscent of many a WWI film. It was widely accepted that the generals of the day cared little for their troops and that casualties were seen only as numbers on a graph somewhere, that had to be less than the other guy's number to be a reliable indicator of 'victory' that day.

As the soldier goes through his meltdown, tortured by images of "bodies filling the fields he sees", he questions why he's there and what he was supposed to be training to fight for, and laments the fact that his life was stolen from him before he even had the chance to really discover it.

The last line of the general's final chorus reveals the true cynicism behind the song as he sneers, "You coward/You servant/You blind man" at the soldier.

Is this James's "us versus them" scenario making a return once more? Or is it merely in keeping with the theme of manipulation that the album has maintained throughout? Certainly "Sanitarium" had hints of that with its unlawfully imprisoned and brutalized protagonist, and again here with the "blind man" reference it is as if the general is laughing at the pointless and stupid sacrifice the soldier has made. He has been ruined without even knowing what he was fighting for, or indeed whether it was even worth fighting for in the first place.

The exploitation of young soldiers is hardly a new thing to songwriting, but this is certainly the finest illustration of such a topic in metal circles, and if James hadn't gone and written "One" it might never have been bettered.

Leper Messiah

During the latter part of the Eighties, rock and metal found itself under a sustained attack from certain quarters of republican society. Not only were the PMRC raising their ugly heads, but an altogether more cynical accuser had stepped up, and that was organized religion. Although Twisted Sister, Ozzy and WASP had deliberately baited the so-called moral majority in order to exploit the surrounding media frenzy for album sales, they – and others like them – had miscalculated the stupidity of the average uninformed Joe as an ever-increasing number of TV preachers emerged to solve the moral ills of society… for a donation to their churches, of course.

Suddenly it seemed as if rock bands *per se* worshipped Satan, and that no child should be allowed within a mile of any heavy metal, lest they become corrupted by the evil powers of the Horned One that must surely lie within their breasts. Unbelievably, these TV preachers were milking literally millions off the broken backs of society's most downtrodden members – those already on the lowest rungs of the ladder of self-esteem, and those who could be manipulated most easily.

Although under attack, there was still a huge backlash from the rock and metal community against these false prophets. Metallica's "Leper Messiah" was one of the first and by far the most articulate to appear, the most noted of the others being Ozzy's "Miracle Man" and, coincidentally, Suicidal Tendencies' brilliant "Send Me Your Money" – which featured the major recording debut of one Robert Trujillo no less.

It's been argued by other writers that "Leper Messiah" is also one of the first examples in song of James's long-held bitterness against organized religion, which, they claim, lies at the root of his sometimes cynical view of the world following the early death of his mother. (As a devout Christian Scientist, she refused medical aid after she contracted cancer when James was a teen.)

It is, of course, possible that "Leper Messiah" does feed from such a long-held resentment and a desire to expose religion as a fraud, but given the command of vocabulary that James had already displayed on the *…Puppets* album I think that if he had chosen to make such an attack it would have been far more obvious and most certainly intended for everyone to understand. Also, and rather more crucially, none of the lyrics Hetfield had thus far produced were ever his internalized thoughts. Not once had there been a genuine first-person lyric penned by Hetfield when he wasn't hiding behind some character he had specifically created to illustrate whatever point he was wishing to make. James simply hadn't reached a level of songwriting maturity at which he would feel comfortable that he could do himself justice, or that he wanted anyone else to have such an insight into his inner thoughts. I would also contend that at this point in his career James didn't yet have self-confidence enough to believe that anything intimate he might choose to write about from the heart would be of interest to anyone else.

Truly personal lyrics, written totally for oneself, are terribly difficult things to release to the public, and many an artist will find it beyond their individual comfort zones or their artistic ability. And for those sort of lyrics to come from Metallica we would have to wait another few years yet.

Orion

It's an instrumental, innit. Damn good one, though. Wickedly strange bass solo.

Damage Inc

There have been many interpretations of just what "Damage Inc" is about. Is it the song of enforcers from some multi-national commercial conglomerate? A Mafia theme song? Or is it just the older, more articulate brother of "Seek And Destroy" – a gleeful expression of violence for violence's sake in a fucked-up amoral world?

Whatever the truth, the moral void in which the character voice operates with its utter lack of concern

Gabba Gabba Hey: The Ramones were no doubt an early influence on James and Lars.

for humanity is simultaneously both chilling and exhilarating. Devilishly, that lack of moral tone is also the most likely source of the song's long-lasting appeal among Metallica speed freaks.

The Mafia link comes from the old "Murder Inc" tag that was used to describe a group of hit-men in Thirties and Forties New York. Legend has it that these individuals were ruthless killers who would often make a gruesome scene of the victim's death in order to add to the intimidation factor among their victims. The actual Murder Inc "gang" were the heads of various crime families who probably never took part in the crimes directly themselves, though they certainly ordered the killings.

Lines such as "All flee, with fear you run/You'll know just where we come from" imply that there is a mission behind the butchery going on, unlike the unreasoning actions of "Battery"'s madman. And the fantastic "Slamming through don't fuck with Razorback" conjures up many an image of a razor blade glinting in the moonlight as it slices down upon some poor unfortunate who has failed to come up with the goods.

The moral void referred to earlier is perfectly executed with the line "Honesty is my only excuse" – a half-hearted attempt on the part of the killer to pass off his crimes.

However, there is an alternative reading of the song that is equally as entertaining as any Mafia theory and which stems from the first verse. Is this a Road Warrior view of a lawless future society, where only the most vicious punks will survive? It certainly talks about going against the grain and being bred to be the biggest bastards in society, but this would necessarily imply an acceptance of anarchy and with lines such as "Stepping out? You'll feel our hell on your back", it seems wishful thinking.

Whatever the truth, the song itself is a minor masterpiece of bile-fuelled hatred. As an album closer it is the perfect partner to the aural assault of "Battery"'s opening charge.

Behind the scenes

Martin Hooker: "*Master of Puppets* went through the roof, charting in every country we released it."

Gem Howard: "'Sanitarium' was a song above its league. You could never imagine Slayer doing that, as much as I love them. No so-called thrash band could write a song like that."

Martin: "When I first heard *Master of Puppets*, I thought it was a masterpiece. They had come on so much. I'd heard some demos but I hadn't heard any finished things until the record landed on my desk. By then Metallica had been signed by a major label – Elektra – in the States and the deal was that if MFN gave them *Ride...* for free then they would pick up all the costs for the recording of *...Puppets*, and we could have that for free across Europe. Ho ho. But the record was amazing, I couldn't believe the scale of what they'd crammed into those eight songs – and you forget that there are only eight tracks on that record in its 55 minutes."

coming on their biggest ever shows – a mid-bill placing in front of 50,000 metal-mad freaks at England's annual Castle Donington "Monsters of Rock" bash and a triumphant homecoming show at Oakland's famed Day on the Green for 60,000 kids – Metallica's hugely anticipated headlining fall tour of Europe in '86 was meant to be a moment of crowning glory. ...*Puppets* was outselling the previous albums three to one, the band had been accepted into the mainstream metal hierarchy when Ozzy had them as support during the summer, and musically Metallica simply couldn't have been a tighter performing unit. But disaster dogged the tour from the outset. A stupid skateboarding accident in late summer left the band using Kirk's guitar tech John Marshall as a stand-in rhythm replacement for a sheepish James Hetfield. But worse was to come.

The night of September 26 was meant to be a celebration – it was James's first gig back on guitar in three months and, as many eye-witnesses would testify, Metallica were raging that night. Support band Anthrax thought that it was one of Metallica's finest ever shows, but as they packed their gear into the back of the truck and bade farewell to the headliners and headed off to Copenhagen for the next show, they had no idea that this had been the last time they would ever set their eyes upon the "classic" Metallica.

The band and four of their crew climbed aboard their roadliner for the overnight drive. Cliff went straight to the far-right top bunk and crashed out, while James, who had been suffering from a sore throat due to the draughty bus and who was due to sleep next to Burton, decided instead to crash in the back lounge, away from the cold. It was a decision that probably saved the singer's life.

At about 6:30am the band were violently awoken by the sound of screeching tyres and the bus lurching toward the right. Taking in the situation quickly, guitar tech John Marshall remembered that the bus had basically swung completely around to face the opposite direction. In the crucial second that the tyres gripped the road the momentum of the spinning bus caused the entire vehicle to flip over on to its right side.

Tour manager Bobby Schneider endured two smashed ribs, Lars a broken foot, Marshall a badly bruised back, while Kirk was briefly knocked unconscious and suffered a black eye. As the walking wounded made their way out of the crash exits it became clear that someone was missing. Kirk was the first to see Cliff's still body pinned halfway under the bus – he had been partly thrown through the bunk window.

Recalled John Marshall: "We were all sitting out there in 35-degree weather, with me in my socks and underwear before someone gave me a blanket. I remember Kirk and James yelling at the driver. By then, everyone had begun to realize that something was wrong with Cliff. I remember James walking up the road a bit to see if there was ice on the road, after the driver had claimed he'd slid over a sheet of ice. Kirk was crying...

"I remember Bobby Schneider lyin' next to me later in the ER, as they were taking blood pressure and stuff, and saying, 'Cliff's gone, you know'. All of a sudden the reality of everything hit me" (3.76).

Cliff's legacy

No matter what anyone else may say there will only ever be one bassist in Metallica, and that man is Cliff Burton. Harsh on the contributions of Jason Newsted and new guy Robert Trujillo? Maybe, but look at the number of songwriting credits given to Burton and compare them against those of Newsted – the numbers speak for themselves.

When Metallica lost Burton they lost the most experimental and musically challenging member of the unit. Cliff's input into the band extended beyond mere riffs or licks – he continually pushed the band forward, and was a passionate defender of Metallica's cutting edge. Had Burton survived you can be sure that the Metallica we have today would be a radically different beast, but also one far less likely to have ascended the commercial heights.

Right: RIP Cliff Burton – The man will always be remembered by all Metallica fans.

A personal look at Cliff

Gem: "Cliff was the one who brought in the musical variation to Metallica. Whereas Lars and James were content listening to NWOBHM stuff day in, day out, Cliff would be in the van listening to The Misfits or The Partridge Family! Cliff didn't give a shit what anyone thought about him, whether it was what he wore or what music he liked – if it worked for him then it was all good. He was a strange one, though. I remember one day we were listening to 'Bridge Over Troubled Water' by Simon And Garfunkel where everyone was singing along, then the tape ended so Cliff flipped in a Misfits one and started banging the shit out of the dashboard like a maniac!

"Y'know, when Cliff died that band were torn to pieces and they seriously did consider splitting up. They truly believed that they'd never replace him, and you know what, no disrespect to Jason Newsted, but they never did. You listen to any of the Jason albums and see if you think he's got a full part in what is going on.

"Metallica grew into a radically different band after Cliff died. I don't think for a second that they would have become a stadium rock band had he still been around, because I don't think he would've thought it was cool. They know that there was a really special chemistry between them when Cliff was around that kept them a cutting-edge band."

Martin: "I got a phone call from the States letting me know (about the accident) and within ten minutes the phones in the office were ringing off the hooks. I just couldn't believe it. It was a complete tragedy. I always thought they'd carry on, but I didn't think that they'd recruit and be comfortable with someone as quickly as they did. It must be very difficult indeed to lose someone like Cliff from such a small tightly knit unit like they were."

Indeed, approaching the eve of release for Metallica's 2003 "comeback" album, *St Anger*, Lars acknowledged to *Metal Hammer* magazine that the three remaining members had, he felt, "punished" Jason for joining the band as a way of dealing with their own survivor guilt issues.

Enter the Jason

'We'll never stop, we'll never quit –
'cause we're Metallica'

("Whiplash")

The band were initially shell-shocked by Cliff's death. James, Lars and Kirk questioned whether they were even a band any more. Yet two weeks after the crash, by the time Cliff's funeral had passed in San Francisco, the Metallica fighting spirit had returned.

In retrospect, their determination to continue was Metallica's way of dealing – or, more accurately, not dealing at all – with the grief of losing their friend. By rushing into auditions for a replacement Metallica were burying themselves in their work and thereby also burying the pain. Work would save them, so they believed.

Many a name bassist tried out for the vacant slot. Some, including Prong's Troy Gregory, came close, but the man they wanted – Armoured Saint's Joey Vera – like his singer before him, turned Metallica down, preferring to stay with his bandmates. Then a phone call came from old friend Brian Slagel that pointed Lars toward a Phoenix-based band called Flotsam And Jetsam, whose curly-haired four-stringer was, in Slagel's opinion, "the business".

Two short rehearsals and one night-long "Alcoholica" session later and Jason Newsted was a firm fixture in his favourite band.

It wasn't at all plain sailing for Jason, though, as the others constantly teased and jibed him whenever the opportunity arose. In the beginning he was even limited on how many press interviews he could do, and it took Newsted years of mental abuse to finally be accepted by the rest of the Metalli-gang. Indeed, it's arguable that Jason never did manage to attain a position of equal level to the others – certainly when it came to songwriting opportunities – something that was clearly hinted at when he announced his decision to move on from Metallica in January of '01.

Far from being a Burton clone Newsted – when publicly allowed – was very much his own man, and toward the end of the *Load/Reload* eras which he found personally frustrating he even cultivated an outspoken voice, one independent of the Metallica party line.

Master of Puppets

Hardly a poor musician even by Metallica's high standards, Jason, rather like former heavyweight boxing champ Larry Holmes who beat the legendary Muhammad Ali, suffered from having simply been unlucky enough to follow in the footsteps of a widely acknowledged genius, whose untimely death spurred the Cult of St Cliff among die-hard fans.

Ironically, and over time, Jason would become a totem of steadfast reliability in the face of the band's cosmetic changes during the *Load/Reload* era. For many die-hard fans through the 1990s it was Jason, not James, that they believed kept the metal in Metallica.

Jason's first photocall. Metallica Mk II hits the road in late '87.

5

...And Justice
For All

Behind the scenes

Gem Howard: "I hated that record – it sounded awful: the bass was non-existent and the drums sounded like biscuit tins. Just goes to show how majors can fuck you up because they can't give you any advice, because they don't understand what you are about."

Martin Hooker: "I was totally gutted when I heard it because I was obviously hoping that *Justice...* would go huge and take the back catalogue with it. When I heard it I almost wept, and it didn't do nearly as well in the UK as it should've done given that the band had three consecutive gold records over here."

'A concept? I don't like that word. A concept to me is something really contrived and premeditated, where you sit down and plan everything out to the smallest detail...The justice thing is just something that fits a lot of the album's lyrical content...'

Lars Ulrich, September 1988 (1.29)

'The fucking thing took two years to make!'

James Hetfield, May 1990 (1.29)

'I feel that (*Justice...*) is the album that has aged least well, but I'm still amazed at some of the playing on it.'

Lars Ulrich, February 1993 (1.33)

'I think the lyrics are really good. I think the production really sucks.'

James Hetfield, November 1992 (1.33)

Lars Ulrich may prefer the world to shy away from seeing *...And Justice For All* as a concept record, and while it's very true that under half of the nine songs on the album directly refer to either corruption in the courts or government manipulation ("...And Justice For All", "Shortest Straw", "Eye Of the Beholder"), such is the power of those tracks, especially when taken in partnership with the album's vivid artwork, which features the blind Lady Justice, that one cannot help but see *Justice...* as a record led by a concept.

The record is also perhaps one of the most difficult that Metallica ever had to record. Amazingly, they managed to write the nine songs in four short weeks, which, as a shocked Lars recalled at the time, was "unheard of in Metallicaland." This was probably due in part to the extra-long lay-off between albums caused by James breaking his arm for a second time in a skateboarding accident, and which had also yielded the stop-gap *$5.98 EP* of Metallisized cover versions.

Unfortunately, initial recording sessions with Guns N' Roses producer Mike Clink did not gel at all, and the

band wasted a month trying to make the process work before re-recruiting long-time producer Flemming Rammussen to the helm. Quite what Flemming brought to the mix is unclear, for as every Metallica fan knows, *Justice...* must feature the worst Metallica production sound ever. And that includes *No Life 'Til Leather*. In fact the whole bottom end of the record was mixed out with the bass being virtually non-existent, and Lars' drums sounding as if they were recorded on empty biscuit tins! The fact that the record was even released at all – sounding, as it does, only partially finished, by agreement with either Q-Prime or the record label, Elektra – speaks volumes about the commercial power that Metallica, or

at least James and Lars anyway, now wielded.

That said, *Justice...* is nevertheless a good Metallica record, and features some of James's hardest hitting lyrics. It also showed that Metallica, who freely acknowledged that they stood upon the precipice of greatness after the commercial success of *...Puppets*, still retained their underground anti-establishment roots by recording their most difficult and inaccessible work to date.

As Metallica saw it, if success was heading their way then it was heading their way on their terms.

...And Justice For All (1988)

Blackened

The natural successor to "Fight Fire With Fire"'s apocalyptic nuclear vision, "Blackened" takes a more rounded but equally as accusatory and nihilistic view that mother Earth is dying through humanity's own greed. By the mid-Eighties the so called "hole" in the ozone layer over Antarctica was big news. Fluorocarbon compounds used in many aerosol sprays are impossible to break down in the atmosphere and this, plus the continued industrial pollution from the burning of fossil fuels in industry and dangerous gas emissions from petrochemicals was, it was argued, accelerating the decay of the ozone layer. Without the ozone layer the Earth would be exposed to the sun's unfiltered UV rays and all life would perish. It was argued by the extreme fringes of Green parties the world over that a poetic justice was being visited upon our heads. The slovenly, greedy way in which western lives consumed natural resources like locusts was now leading to the threat of our very extinction. Since then there have been many other theories put forward as to why the hole appeared over Antarctica, but undoubtedly the use of fossil fuels continues to make an impact.

It is unlikely that James had suddenly turned into a new age eco-warrior and felt compelled to write about our imminent destruction; instead, like Ozzy Osbourne, who has written a number of sentimental pro-Earth tunes, the Metallica man probably found the example of being able to graphically demonstrate man's stupidity and selfishness too much of an opportunity to pass up.

As Lars summed up at the time: "It's just about all the shit that's going on in the world right now, and how the whole environment that we're living in is slowly deteriorating into a shithole. This is not meant to be a huge environment statement or anything like that, it's just a harsh look at what's going on around us." (1.29).

James is quite graphic in his description of the choking earth, citing the pollutants of "deadly nicotine" and goes on to name-check the mountains of discarded freezer units with their deadly insoluble fluorocarbons

James's guitar says it all.

with the lines "Callous frigid chill/Nothing left to kill".

As the song progress it also becomes clear that James is attacking the political process by which these Green crimes are allowed to occur. A list of words familiar to us all as the language of the politician and his procrastinating rhetoric is barked out as a roll-call of shame: "Opposition, contradiction, premonition, compromise/Agitation, violation, mutilation, planet dies". James's point is simple: while we sit around waiting for politicians to half-heartedly lobby for whatever minuscule cuts in pollution that their industry paymasters in the giant companies will superficially agree to, the planet will continue to die, and so will we.

...And Justice For All

James's finger of accusation is squarely pointed at America's justice system here. To the Metallica mindset there is no liberty and justice for all to be found in the courts of the USA – it's liberty and justice for those who can afford it. For a song written in 1988 now that we are post-OJ Simpson, consider how much of this bitter sentiment rings true. "Halls of Justice painted green" starts the song, making a clear reference to how money paves the way to liberty for some. The adversarial judicial procedures adopted by US courts is not interested in finding out facts or proving the acts a crime at all, it is a system supposedly built upon finding someone guilty or not guilty of the crime they are accused of. There is a major difference therefore – truth isn't the desired outcome – as James so neatly hits the mark, "Seeking no truth/The winning is all" and the hard verse: "Truth assassin/Rolls of red tape seal your lips/Now you're done in/Their money tips her scales again".

When describing the song before its release Lars said, "It's about the court systems in the US where it seems like no one is ever concerned with finding out the truth any more. It's becoming more and more like one lawyer versus another-type situation, where the best lawyer can alter justice any way he wants" (1.29).

Seeing how James's lyric develops he could well have a particular case in mind, one in which a multi-national company has paid expensive lawyers to defend against the claim of an individual who is clearly not going to win against such formidable opposition, no matter how guilty they may be.

The song/album title "...And Justice For All" actually comes from a 1979 satirical movie of the same name by director Norman Jewison. James went on record as stating that he was struck by the sick way the judicial system went all-out to trample the rights of the film's protagonist in the interests of chasing the big green bucks (2.126).

The curtailment or abuse of individual freedoms is a recurring theme throughout this album's songs. Both "Eye Of The Beholder" and "Shortest Straw" directly address this issue, as would "Don't Tread On Me" later on.

Like many of the tracks on the album, the impact of "...And Justice For All" seems diluted by the dreary length of the song, a fact compounded by the deliberately bone-dry production. A few years later even James Hetfield agreed things hadn't gone to plan, saying, "I think that the songs are good, but I think we got a little too fancy with shit. I think there's some good riffs on there, but they're spoiled by the length of the songs." (1.33).

Eye of the Beholder

In typical Metallica fashion, this is James once more standing up for the rights of the little man being bullied by the government. "It's about people interfering with your way of thought, and how America is really not as free as people think," observed Lars (1.32).

This time though, James had taken inspiration from one particular incident that he felt personally affected by. In the mid-Eighties seminal Californian punks The Dead Kennedys had been dragged through the US courts because of the "obscene" nature of their 1985 *Frankenchrist* EP, which featured art by controversial surrealist Swiss artist HR Giger (he of *Alien/Poltergeist II*

The incredible Lady Justice stage set in full glory.

fame). His work, dubbed "Penis landscape", was used as a free poster inside the album sleeve, but was still considered too offensive by the federal government to be distributed – it branded the artwork (and by default the band) "pornographic and obscene". The Dead Kennedys' flamboyant singer and main activist, Jello Biafra (appearing under his real name Eric Boucher), was charged with "distributing harmful materials to minors" after the mother of a teenage DK fan was outraged by the poster and complained to the authorities. The singer faced a maximum $2,000 fine or one year in prison.

Fortunately for Biafra, who acquitted himself brilliantly in court, the end result was a hung jury and there was no re-trial. Unfortunately for The Dead Kennedys, the financial strain of mounting the defence sunk the band and (albeit only briefly) Alternative Tentacles (the record company that they owned) too, and they broke up amid accusations that Biafra had chosen the court route as a means of self-publicity to make a political point.

"What do you think is art? What's pornography? What's brilliant? Just what's in your head?" asked James of *Circus* magazine in 1988, when talking about the song. "You can't express yourself the way you want. It's kinda scary. I mean, you've got a choice – if you don't want to look at it, don't look at it" (2.126).

The cutting lyrics that a steely voiced Hetfield unleashes must rank among his most venomous: "Do you hear what I hear?/Doors are slamming shut/Limit your imagination, Keep you where they must/Do you feel what I feel?/Bittering distress/Who decides what you express?"

As an anti-censorship lyric written in defence of the freedom of expression it ranks as one of the better ones to come out of the metal fraternity, alongside Megadeth's 1987 anti-PMRC tirade "Hook In Mouth". Years later it would take Marilyn Manson an entire album, *Holy Wood (In the Valley of the Shadow of Death)*, to make the same point, and even then it's arguable that many missed it.

The music throughout "Eye Of The Beholder" is a bullish, almost military stop/start arrangement, full of pointed threats and implied violence, with James's guitar sounding particularly vengeful throughout. And not a single penis landscape in sight.

One

The unofficial heart of the album, "One" succeeds as a song where "...And Justice For All" does not, primarily because of the haunting nature of the song's narrator. Unlike the dry rant of "Justice", which carries the weight of the album's name, "One" is very much off-message for such a politically themed album. Much to James's chagrin many Metallica fans still erroneously believe that "One" is some extravagant and deliberately poignant anti-war song.

Without doubt the song is poignant, made more so by the disturbing nature of the accompanying video (the first that the band ever agreed to make), but it was never intended to be any sort of grand statement.

As Lars admitted at the time: "It's about someone who has no limbs, no speech, no sight, no hearing and is basically a living brain. It's about what sort of thoughts you would have if you were placed in that situation. It's actually a lyrical idea that we had a couple of years ago, bit we never got around to using it before" (1.32).

The concept of "One" appealed to Metallica as horror junkies, fascinated and intrigued by the "what if?" and gross-out factors rather than because they were in any way passionate anti-war campaigners. As Lars indicated, they'd had the idea kicking around for years, but just hadn't developed it any further.

After enduring a couple of years' worth of undeserved platitudes for the contribution to the anti-war movement, it finally caught up with the band while they were on tour in Italy in '91. Lars remembers: "...there were these two guys just drilling into this whole thing about 'One' and anti-war, and making a statement of peace for the kids. 'You guys care so much'. I was telling James about this afterwards. We were laughing, 'Why do people make such a big deal about it?' And James turns around and goes, 'All it is, is a big fucking song about a guy who steps on a landmine!' That kinda sums the whole thing up' (1.36).

Of course, Metallica only have themselves to blame for any misunderstandings, and the Machiavellian side to Mr Ulrich would not have failed to notice that "One"s success on MTV and its subsequent radio play (another first for a Metallica track) was largely due to the sense of empathy that listeners felt with the tragic horror that had befallen the song's narrator.

"One"s accompanying video flits from the grainy black-and-white acoustic beginnings to the gory shrapnel-filled scenes of the later full-on thrash metal parts, and is littered with scenes lifted from the 1970 cult classic film *Johnny Got His Gun*, by Dalton Trumbo. One key scene may in fact lie at the root of the song's misreading, and that is where young protagonist Joe Bonham asks his father what democracy is and his father replies that democracy is something "that any father would gladly give up his only son to die for". The film goes on to show Joe being recruited to fight in WWI and stepping on a landmine that renders him blind, mute and a limbless stump, able to communicate only by morse code. From his dark sensory deprived hell Joe finally hits upon the idea of asking the nurses to kill him and end his misery.

In the ecstasy of finding footage that would dramatize the impact of "One"s lyrical concept better than they could have ever hoped, Metallica actually changed the message that their fanbase heard. Thank God.

The Shortest Straw

According to manager Cliff Bernstein, Metallica had the title "Shortest Straw" and the vague concept outline involving members of society forced to draw a "shortest straw" in a lottery-type way, before they had any real lyrics or even music to speak of!

Bernstein recommended that James read Victor Navasky's *Naming Names* and Norman Mailer's *The Deer Park*, both novels written in the 1950s at the height of the McCarthy witch-hunts in Hollywood. At the time the FBI, under the omnipotent control of J Edgar Hoover and at the direction of Senator Joe McCarthy, were tearing through the movie industry like an evil wind, desperate to "out" communist sympathisers whom they believed to be lurking within Hollywood's more cosmopolitan folds. In the end several directors, producers and actors were officially blacklisted and imprisoned, while dozens more were discredited by government-organized whispering campaigns, and subsequently disowned by movie studios fearful of federal retribution. Perhaps the worst facet of this sick witch-hunt was the fact that having caught one "subversive" the FBI would coerce him or her into turning traitor on friends and colleagues before letting them go free. Then, regardless of whether they had helped with enquiries or not, it would be made known they had complied with the investigation, thereby ruining their credibility overnight.

The idea of the social outcast removed from their original place in society by shadowy forces appealed to

Lars spots a rabid chipmunk and recoils in terror.

the band's sense of championing the underdog.

As Lars said at the time, "'Shortest Straw' deals with the whole blacklisting thing that took place in the Fifties, where anyone whose view was a little out of the ordinary was immediately labelled as a potential threat to society. There were all these people in Hollywood whose views didn't fit in with the mainstream, and they were all shoved out of the entertainment industry because of their beliefs' (1.29).

Knowing this makes the lyrics' reading clearer, as James stands finger-pointing at the culprits, much as if he had lifted a rock and the bugs had scattered at the sight of daylight: "The accusations fly/Discrimination, why?/Your inner self to die/Intruding/Doubt sunk itself in you."

Thematically, then, "Shortest Straw" fits right in alongside the album's title track and "Eye Of The Beholder", warning of government abuses of power and wary of the loss of one's rights when faced by the awesome machinery of the establishment.

Musically, the song is an up-tempo thrasher in the finest traditions of Metallica, as it delivers a much-needed boost of energy to the album's flagging middle section.

Harvester of Sorrow

"Harvester..." can be seen as the grown-up cousin to *Master of Puppets* rage anthem "Battery". As Lars revealed, "It's about someone who leads a normal 9–5 life, has a wife and three kids, and all of a sudden, one day, he just snaps and starts killing people around him. It's not a pretty subject, I guess..." (1.29)

In modern society we feel secure in the strength of our national defences and our strength of will to defend ourselves against those who would challenge our way of life. In fact, pre-9/11, the only one true fear that we had was that which came from within. If one of our own, a trusted member of our society, goes apeshit with a gun then our world turns almost upside down. For if it can happen to your next-door neighbour, maybe it can happen to you also. Then there are the questions of why

you work so hard for so little reward. Why you don't get any respect from the kids over the road that you damn well deserve. And then there's that boss of yours, he's a real prick, doesn't he know how much money you make for him? What's that? You've been fired because of your shitty attitude? And there's a goddamn parking ticket and Jesus Christ, some kid has graffitied the car trunk and the wife has run off with a secondhand car dealer you used to beat up at school...

Metallica's "Harvester of Sorrow" is a sadly prophetic character as much as he is a horror movie-type gross-out. Madmen on the rampage have become a worrisome fact of life for many western societies – Michael Ryan in Hungerford; Thomas Hamilton in Dunblane; Columbine – the list goes on, but equally they are prime macabre fodder for the twistedly aggressive sounds generated by a band that sounds like Metallica.

"Harvester..." was released ahead of the album in the UK as a single, and featured two Metallica soundcheck faves as B-sides that had failed to make it on to the *$5.98 EP*. The first was Diamond Head's "The Prince" and the second Budgie's "Breadfan", which, due to fan demand, would soon be included in the Metallica live set, the latter's central tune being the finest riff James Hetfield never wrote.

The Frayed Ends of Sanity

Like "Welcome Home (Sanitarium)" before it, "Frayed Ends..." deals with someone who is losing a grip on their mind. The eerily distorted vocal line – deliberately ripped straight from *The Wizard of Oz* – adds to the sense of mounting dementia, and it is by far the most atmospheric of any song included on this most barren of (un)produced records.

Imagined people in extreme mental conditions appeal to Hetfield as lyrical subjects only because they fit the extreme nature of the music being written. It's highly unlikely James hangs out in sanitariums checking out the next basket case to help him past his writer's block (though you never can be sure) but, if we're honest, there's a little bit in all of us fascinated by the freak.

Ever developing as a lyricist, James employs a particularly effective yet subtle trick in the second verse in order to convince the listener that they are indeed bearing witness to a mind out of touch with itself. Following the lines "I'm the slave of fear, My captor/ Never warnings/Spreading its wings" there is a crucial moment when the narrator refers to that "fear" as a separate sentient entity rather than an emotion generated from within, when he says, "As I wait for the horror she brings..." In the mind of narrator, then, there are demons at work ripping apart all sense of the normal, and as the depression kicks in James dramatizes the moment with the lines, "Into Ruin/I am sinking/ Hostage to this nameless feeling..." Never one to truly meld with James's lyrics, Lars observed that "Frayed..." was, "just about paranoia – you know, being afraid, but not really knowing what you are afraid of" (1.32).

To Live is to Die

Including music and lyrics written by Cliff some time after the recording of ...Puppets was obviously a real gamble for Metallica. Sensitive to accusations of exploiting the memory of 'the dead one' for album sales on one hand and, one had to assume, careful not to overshadow the contribution and existence of the new recruit, Jason Newsted, the band were really trapped between a rock and hard place. In the end common sense prevailed – the material Cliff had left behind was simply too good to waste and every note of it was pure Metallica.

As Lars noted, "A lot of people might give us flak about this because it features some riffs written by Cliff a few months before he was killed – just like they gave us flak about using Mustaine's stuff – but the truth of the matter is, these riffs were just so huge and

Metallica-sounding we had to use them. We're certainly not trying to dwell on Cliff's death or anything, we're simply using the best ideas we had available, and this was one of them" (1.32). "To Live Is To Die" was the most adventurous instrumental the band had recorded, a mini-symphony in effect, and when it came to the final version there were some 15 separate guitar tracks featured in the mix and (shock!) a blues solo recorded by Kirk!

Dyer's Eve

The fastest and, oddly, the most progressive track on the album, "Dyer's Eve" very nearly didn't even make it to the studio as it was the very last song to be written. Metallica's insistence upon its inclusion forced the record company to press ...And Justice For All as a double-vinyl album in order to contain its 65 minutes of music.

The lyrics are self-explanatory, as Lars stated at the time: "It's basically about this kid who's been hidden from the real world by his parents the whole time he was growing up, and now that he's out there he can't cope with it and is contemplating suicide.

"It's basically a letter from this kid to his parents asking them why they didn't expose him to the real world and why they kept him hidden for so long" (1.32).

Indeed, it was Lars who came up with the title for "Dyer's Eve", recalling the 1970 Dustin Hoffman movie *Little Big Man*, in which Hoffman's on-screen grandfather announces that, "Today would be a good day for dying." Lars held on to the phrase and questioned James whether the kid writing the letter in his new song was approaching it from a "dyer's eve", especially if he were looking at the very next day as being his last.

It is also possible that much of the frustrations being vented in the song's letter were taken directly from James Hetfield's own life. In Chris Cocker's book *Frayed Ends of Metal*, James Hetfield recalls a Christian Scientist family boasting that their daughter had broken her arm had healed herself through God, and everything was now fine. Looking at the girl's mangled, useless arm, the young James felt that everything was definitely not OK.

James Hetfield: metal god.

6
Metallica

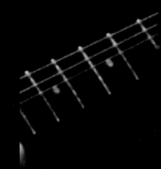

Bob Rock

Prior to his stint as "the man who made Metallica big", Bob Rock already had an impressive résumé to his name. Scarcely an album Rock had touched failed to go platinum, and, given some of the ropey names on that list that success speaks volumes! Kingdom Come and Blue Murder were the lesser-known successes but The Cult, Bon Jovi and Mötley Crüe need no introduction to any rock fan. Regardless of what the band thought of any of the cock-rockers on the list, Metallica definitely heard enough in what Rock had achieved for those bands to invite him into their tightly knit lives. Kirk made no secret that, as a long time Cult fan, he had much admiration for Rock's sonic ear, while even James had words of praise for the punch of Mötley's guitar sound that Rock captured on their massive-selling *Dr Feelgood* record and in typical grudging Hetfieldian manner commented, "...if you go back and look at the stuff he's produced, it sounds great, even though the songs were crap and the bands were fucking gay!" (1.47)

So what did Bob Rock bring to the band? Says Lars: "Bob has an incredible ear for attitude and feeling. Now that we've worked with him on pre-production, he's got us kicking ourselves for not doing certain things sooner." (1.36), while Kirk admitted that Bob had encouraged him to approach his solos differently, saying, "I'd listen to the song, and instead of sitting down with the guitar I'd sing out ideas into my tape recorder." (1.43)

Basically, Bob expanded Metallica's vision of what they could accomplish as a band, and encouraged them to not only experiment with new ideas but also to simplify their sound. Where previously the band had jammed as many riffs into one song as they could manage – extending the song to be eight, nine, or even ten minutes if they felt like it – Rock encouraged them to whittle the excess away and distill the energy – the pure essence of Metallica – into one riff per song. It worked.

Concert followed concert followed concert to support the Black album.

Metallica (1991)

'We definitely put 110 per cent into this one, and that's what we got out.'

James Hetfield, November 1992

Every band dreams of having a successful career, maybe – they hope – if they're lucky, they'll also score a couple of big hits and ensure that they retain a fan base that will keep them alive in their twilight years. No band ever truly believes that they will record the biggest album of the year. Or the decade.

Metallica, the 'black' album, the snake album or whatever you wish to call it, changed everything for Metallica. The band went from good-selling next-big-things to becoming a mammoth outfit with incredible commercial opportunities. The record's five singles – "Enter Sandman", "Wherever I May Roam", "Sad But True", "The Unforgiven" and the huge "Nothing Else Matters" may have each drawn in new crowds unfamiliar with Metallica's dark hue, but they were hardly "popular" singles in the Def Leppard or Bon Jovi league. Nope, *Metallica* sold over ten million copies upon the strength of the whole album, and while the band's already existing fan base certainly propelled them through the first million-odd units, after that it was down to the sheer hard road work endured by the band. And the quality of those 310 shows ensured that there was no such thing as a potential Metallica fan – you either were or were never, ever gonna be.

Enter Sandman

"'Enter Sandman' is quite the simplest song we've ever written. If you look at the song closely there's really only one riff in it. The whole song is written around one riff. Which, I think, is an incredible thing to say about a Metallica song!" (1.47)

"Enter Sandman" might well have featured the simplest of riffs for a Metallica song but Lars could just have easily been talking up the simplest of James's lyrics. The last five years of lyrical Metallidom had been ruled by paranoia, dementia and legal corruption, and yet here came an almost childlike bedtime rhyme, set to an anthemic chest-beating rhythm tailor-made for arenas and festival grounds the world over.

Once again, it's easy to accuse Metallica of a "sell out", but given that the band have metamorphosed into a

Left: James cultivates his wildman look.

Opposite: Don't tread on me! The snake pit takes form.

different animal with every album release you'd have to start wondering what the hell they'd have left to actually sell by now! In fact, in lyrical terms at least, "Enter Sandman" is as much a return to "the old school" as anything the band had committed to album since *Kill 'Em All*. A line such as: "Dreams of war, dreams of liars/Dreams of dragon's fire/And of things that will bite" wouldn't have been out of place in either "No Remorse" or "Phantom Lord", though we can certainly believe that the 18-year-old Hetfield who wrote the lyrics to those particular former classics would've been struggling with the both the superb vocal melody of their modern cousin, and the concepts of fairytale and myth that run through what became Metallica's first true worldwide hit.

Stylistically then, the song is classic Metallica no matter how accessible the chorus – it's about impending doom approaching over the horizon, and the inner demons of the mind waiting to break free. The clever concession James makes to the song is to refrain from over-dramatizing the scenario, and instead of trying to 'explain' madness and fear through the eyes of a madman à la "Sanitarium" or "Harvester of Sorrow", he instead opts to speak as a child. The fears and horrors we experience as children are often imprinted upon our psyches for life – a chance encounter with an aggressive dog as a kid can often put someone off canines for ever, never mind any mention of slugs or spiders!

Essentially, James is taking us all back to our impressionable infant minds, when the scariest things in life hide under the bed or in the closet, which somehow never seems to close properly. The literal inclusion of the night-time prayer in the third chorus is a gleefully wicked yet masterful stroke, as it provides the song with a much-needed respite before launching into the final chorus attack.

It has been mooted on various Metallica fan sites that James might have been influenced to write the song after having read one of writer Neil Gaiman's hugely popular *Sandman* comics. In Gaiman's fantasy world "the Sandman" is a very real person, or rather a god – one of the seven so called "Endless" who govern/serve/facilitate humanity, depending which character perspective you

ultimately believe. As the lord of the dream world, the Sandman can move through, manipulate, even terrorize anyone's dreams where all things are possible. At the turn of the Nineties, Gaiman's comic collections were selling to the newly discovered mature reader market in their hundreds of thousands, richly decorated by cover artist Dave McKean who would go on to create some of the most eye-catching metal album covers of the decade (Machine Head's *Burn My Eyes*, Fear Factory's *Demanufacture* etc., etc.). Indeed, metal legend Alice Cooper would commission Gaiman/McKean to write the plot and backstory to his 1994 epic *The Last Temptation*, which also appeared in comic format on shelves alongside the record. But was James Hetfield a fan? Well, James has never been one to shy away from comic culture – after all, he was the driving force behind commissioning skate artist Pushead in the mid-Eighties – but given James's penchant for externalized characters and their worlds, it would be more than a little strange that at the height of his lyrical powers he would choose to only now base his lyrics on a comic book character. Adding to this scepticism is the fact that long-time friends of Metallica, Anthrax – the band who at one time hardly ever shied away from any comic book character – were experiencing a huge backlash from fans against that very concept, having been outed as "one trick ponies". James set out to write a simple song about nightmares, and nightmares are kids' stuff we can all relate to.

Sad but True

Certainly a perspective song, as it almost reads as a monologue being dictated to the listener via the mouth of James Hetfield, however there is a subtle change in the delivery. Where once James would have made it very clear that the narrator was just a character by referring to something concrete in the real world, in this song here is none of that reassurance – it's simply a voice in your head: "You! You're my mask/My cover/My shelter/You!/You're the one who's blamed". It could just

The band's image changed with their successes of the 1990s.

Metallica

Lean, Mean, Guitar Machine: Hetfield entertains the troops.

be another trip into the mind of a schizo à la "Frayed Ends Of Sanity", but having done such a good job only one album earlier it's highly unlikely. Maybe then this is one of the very first examples of the "real" James Hetfield confronting his own demons. Performers of all types readily admit that they assume a character, a persona if you will, while they are on stage or conducting interviews in order to deal with the intense experience of performance and expectation, and this could be Hetfield's own inner voice eating away at his insecurities, making him go through the motions of being "the singer in Metallica".

James coming clean is one way of reading the song, but there is another – that James is just externalizing the very intimate fears and jealousies that each one of us goes through in our daily lives. Each one of us has lied to someone else to either make ourselves feel better or escape responsibility of some sort and, furthermore, each time we do it we know we're doing wrong yet often we'll make a very private deal with ourselves to pay some form of penance at some other time. Lying to a friend or lover one day might well be offset by helping an old lady

across the road the next, though we don't always feel better about having done the former when going to bed that night. James may well be taking those everyday regrets that we all get and visualizing them as a separate personality that can represent the everyday darker side of human nature.

However, given that this is Metallica, and that the music comes at a crushingly heavy volume, it is also more than fitting that these everyday mistakes and corruptions are presented as the building blocks of something more sinister. As the song builds towards the end and the lyrics unfold, the concepts of jealousy and scapegoats give way to harsher ones such as hate, paying the price for your actions and the need for alibis. James is saying, "Hey, this is what we are. Look at yourself when you see all the hurtful or violent things that others do and ask whether you really are so different, 'cause I know I'm not."

Sad, but definitely true.

Holier than Thou

Certainly the fastest and most traditional Metallica-sounding track on the album, "Holier Than Thou", perhaps rarely for a James lyric, also has its roots in a very real-life scenario. While every band will freely admit that the few precious hours they spend onstage are better than any drug in the world, the more level-headed bands will also readily admit that the touring cycle contains just as many boring oft-repeated regimes as it does orgasmic highs. For many artists, coming off stage and into the dressing room on such a high is one of the hardest parts of the job, because once you're off stage and out of the adulation, how do you maintain it?

Partying after the show is as much a part of the band experience as the performance. Most bands accept that creating a successful act the size of Metallica is a team effort involving various different businesses, from record companies to promoters and agents, local radio and press. All of these different "teams" need to be thanked, spoken to and groomed by the band or their organization to keep everyone sweet. For the people in the bands it's often where the real bad rock star attitude comes from, as it's easy to believe one hundred strangers each telling you that you were "so wonderful tonight" when in fact you know that you missed several notes, that the onstage sound was a mess, and your voice was screwed from the second song in.

Drugs are plentiful in the rock star's world if they choose to let them in, and so are the pushers or "faces" who always find an in with someone on the venue or roadcrew payroll. Rapidly the backstage areas of most large city gigs will turn into a free-for-all of faces determined to push into the band's life. Add to that local radio pluggers, record company execs introducing their friends to "their buddies in Metallica", eager journalists, old "friends" that the band haven't seen in years, the obligatory groupies, and pretty soon the backstage is a veritable menagerie of half-truths and bullshit.

It's this chaos that every band landing on the major

gig circuit will, at some point, step into, but when that band is Metallica, with its wide range of personalities, then resentment will brew. For example, Lars and Kirk like to party, Jason talks business and James, until he quit drinking in '01, just hated the whole thing, preferring to drink with a select few "real" friends until he fell over.

"Holier Than Thou" is a song written about the type of people that would infuriate James when he found himself trapped in that backstage scene. Even producer – and regular party fiend himself – Bob Rock considered James's acidic lyrics to be too close to home for comfort, as the singer recalled in 1991: "When I brought in the lyrics to 'Holier Than Thou', Bob said, 'Hey, is this about me?' He got real paranoid. It's more or less the typical rock ligging that goes on. Slipping in through the door because of name-dropping and shit like that" (1.47).

Indeed, the opening verse sets out all that anyone needs to know about James's feelings on the matter – "No More! The crap slips out your mouth again/Haven't changed, your brain is still gelatin/Little whispers circle around your head/Why don't you worry about yourself instead?"

Backstage tales of drugs 'n' debauchery are legion within rock circles, whether it be apocryphal tales of Led Zeppelin and red snappers or Ozzy Osbourne snorting a line of ants while dressed in his wife's skirt. Though Metallica have certainly indulged in more than a few wild parties of their own, they've never publicly gone over the top, largely one feels by virtue of their own even-measured minds rather than any wary managers keeping a watchful eye. Indeed, the trappings of the everyday rock star seem to actively irk James and Jason, particularly on the huge Metallica/GN'R stadium tour of '93 when the twosome took to defacing Lars' very rock star-ish white-leather-fringed GN'R jacket! It seems as though for every escalation in their world, one or more of them has privately battled against it. When it became clear that the band could now afford their own Lear jet to fly between gigs, Jason would often opt out, preferring the comfort and camaraderie of the road crew.

Given the high-level touring life of Metallica it's no wonder that they came up with the song, and it's actually much more of a surprise that every band hasn't written its own "Holier Than Thou"!

The Unforgiven

Without doubt, "The Unforgiven" is one of the most complete songs that Metallica have ever written. Bob Rock's insistence that the band treat James's singing voice as an instrument, and approach songwriting based around vocal melodies as much as his battering riffs, was central to the creation of this song.

As James recalled in 1991: "'The Unforgiven' is one of my favourite tracks on the album. It's about a guy who never really takes advantage of certain situations, never really takes any chances. Then, later on in his life, he regrets not having done anything with his life, so he dubs the rest of the world 'the unforgiven'. There's a simple aspect to a lot of the songs on this album, and those were pretty hard on us to write. We can write the hundred-riffs-in-one-minute songs, but our challenge this time was to write a simple song and make it mean and thick as shit" (1.43).

Within its five minutes "The Unforgiven" shows just what a complex and mature outfit Metallica had become, taking the audience from the crunch of the guitar that reflects the grinding drudgery of his daily life to the inner beauty and lost hope reflected by the plaintive lines, "What I've felt/What I've known/Never shined through in what I've known".

This is Hetfield's writing taking a clear leap into the unknown. As much as Metallica were pushing the boundaries of what they themselves were prepared to achieve with the record sonically, it seems James was now fully prepared to take stock of his own internal feelings and fears, and finally lay them out for the world to see. Everyone has moments of regret, and fears that when our final days come we'll look back and wish we'd done more. James's twist on this is to portray a man old enough to know that he's still got a few more years left in which to hate the world for what he's allowed it to do to himself and ask us, "just how much of

Wherever They May Roam: Yet another gig for the band.

him do you fear you'll become?"

Like "Nothing Else Matters", "The Unforgiven" is hated by many hardcore Metalli-heads as it concentrates on the overtly commercial qualities of the band's music and, for them, epitomizes the "sell-out metal band" tag. What the hardcore fail to understand is that if Metallica had written a ballad in the truest sense it would sound sod all like this one – it would sound like "Mama Said" on *Load*.

The power in "The Unforgiven" is within its haunting, melancholic quality, which James's almost wistful voice captures perfectly ahead of the violent swing of the central riff. If anything, "The Unforgiven" epitomizes exactly how skilled a set of songwriters they had become, and how perfectly in tune with people's lives James's lyrics were.

Wherever I May Roam

At some point in a long career every senior rock band will write a celebratory on-the-road song, not only because it's always going to be a crowd-winner at shows but also because touring is what people in bands do for so much of their lives! For Metallica, who completed 275 shows on the "Damaged Justice" tour and who were looking at over 300 more as a follow-up on the next, touring was just a fact of life.

As Kirk recalled in 1992: "One person started complaining about his personal life, and then another person said, 'Well, I'm having problems too.' And then a third person said, 'Well, goddman it, I am too!' It wasn't something that was influenced by each other at all. And when we were having these problems with our personal lives it made us realize how much of a foundation the band is for us" (1.53).

Not only does "Wherever I May Roam" connect the band to each other but like another classic road-life song, Motörhead's "(We Are) The Road Crew", it also re-affirms and celebrates the bond between band and their fans who have been with them on those journeys.

Of equal note and interest is the confidence on display by the band being comfortable with recording a song that isn't about a dark subject at all. No dementia, death, war, corruption, lies, regrets or nightmares are to be found within the camaraderie of "Wherever I May Roam". By taking this step Metallica, either by accident or by design, were also cutting the final links with any sort of "extreme" or "underground" or "fringe" tag. Like every other rock 'n' roll band they were now writing about being a rock'n'roll band and not just a scary, loud, heavy metal monster.

The song certainly captures the outlaw spirit that is so attractive to us all, with its: "… The road becomes my bride/…The Earth becomes my throne/… And my ties are severed clean" intro lines to each verse. Just how many of us have wished that we could each pack all that we need into a bag and walk out of our regular lives to become someone else? It's a classic anti-hero folk tale of non-responsibility, and it's no wonder that many Hell's Angels the world over have adopted it as an unofficial anthem to rival that of Motörhead's "Iron Horse".

The video that the band made to accompany it was a typical on-the-road montage comprising hand-held camera and off-duty footage that placed the band firmly in the lineage of Bon Jovi's "Wanted Dead Or Alive", GN'R's "Paradise City" and Mötley Crüe's "Home Sweet Home" – all monster-sized MTV hits trading off the vagabond cartoon nature of life on the road. If it wasn't clear to people now then it never would be – Metallica weren't taking on the mainstream, they had waited 'til they became the mainstream.

Don't Tread on Me

At the time this was to become the most controversial song Metallica had ever released. With war having broken out in the Persian Gulf for the first time between Allied forces and Saddam Hussein's invading Iraqi army, "Don't Tread On Me" was identified by the give-peace-a-chance liberals as an anti-war song.

The liberals were arguing (much as they would 12 years later) that military intervention was unnecessary and that the US government's decision to send in troops was undemocratic. On the surface of things Metallica, who had broken through with a seemingly anti-war anthem in "One" three years previously, now had a new song called "Don't Tread On Me" with a pastiche intro taken from West Side Story's "I Want To Live In America" tune. Surely then this was the band to take up the "not in my name" mantle? Wrong! Metallica's rejection of the left wing suddenly turned into a full-scale backlash as media institutions the world over now chose to see Metallica's song as some sort of jingoistic war dance. Recalled James in '92:

"We never hopped onto any bandwagon when war started. People see the word 'war' in a song and freak. We were getting calls to do that 'Give Peace A Chance' video. Peace off, motherfucker! If you ask me, I don't think this band was really against this war. When I told people that, they freaked. Especially the ones who wanted us to do that video.

"It's like the trend was all hippy, dippy, peace, love, this and that. But then, when we started crushing the Iraqis, people got all patriotic all of a sudden. And I thought, 'Yeah OK, as long as it's a blowout, cool. As long as our guys don't die, fuck it!'

"… In the song it says 'war', but the line is 'to secure peace is to prepare for war', which is a quote from the 1780s, or something. It's basically about how the snake became the logo" (1.53).

"Don't Tread On Me" isn't any pro-Gulf war anthem at all, and even though many a Metallica insignia has been adopted by US troops in many a conflict since then, Metallica can't really be held responsible for the actions of pumped-up GIs.

As James inferred in the last quote, "Don't Tread On Me" is actually taken from the snake symbol/warning sign of the same name that was the insignia of famous West Virginia revolutionaries The Culpeper Minutemen. It was an expression of defiance and in homage to their spirit, not an exhortation to all-out war.

As James indicated one of the central tenets of the Culpeper credo was the idea that peace could be secured through strength. To accuse Metallica, of all

bands, of being pro-war after four albums of cynical anti-authoritarianism is more than a bit ironic. But as James was at pains to point out to *Spin* magazine at the time: "On '…And Justice For All' we stayed to the shitty side – not 'America sucks' but we pointed out the scary parts. But certain people, they're way out of hand with that sort of shit. Go fucking somewhere else, man."

Kirk, speaking to the influential street/skate mag, *Thrasher*, went even further: "That tune had been around a long time before anybody even knew who Saddam Hussein was. A lot of people misinterpreted that as being a pro-war song like, 'Let's go out there and kick some ass'… it was a huge misunderstanding based on a very wrong assumption. People are quick to assume things. I'm not for war in any shape or form; I'm pretty much a chicken shit."

Once again people had judged Metallica with their preconceptions and once again, frustratingly, Metallica refused to play anyone's game save their own. On one side they had certainly raged at authority and used the horrors of war to illustrate their dark soundscapes so, the thinking followed, it was only natural to assume the band's anti-war status. On the other hand, for them to suddenly reject such a notion outright made Metallica look like little more than a bunch of survivalist-like rednecks railing against any government authority, especially when knowledge of Hetfield's passion for hunting alongside red-hot NRA/Republican-stalwart rocker Ted Nugent became popular knowledge.

To add insult to injury, all Hetfield was actually trying to do in his song was to celebrate the spirit of the common man – exactly as he had done on numerous previous occasions. Standing up for oneself and one's rights is the basis of the US constitution, and although a patriotic sentiment, it is hardly jingoistic, despite the fact that US Army types have, on occasion, adopted the song as an anthem.

Metallica weren't the first, and certainly will not be the last, heavy rock band to be judged harshly under the heavily politicized eye of the modern media.

Lars Just Wants To Have Fun…

Through the Never

If "Through the Never" had been written for *Ride the Lightning*, you can be sure that James's take on the lyrical perspective would have involved riding a flame-tailed comet as it plunged into Earth and wiped out humanity. A *Master of Puppets*-era song might well have spoken from the point of view of being on Earth looking upwards and seeing impending doom in all its apocalyptic glory raining down upon us.

The point is that by the time of actually writing "Through The Never" in 1991 Hetfield had reached a lyrical maturity to match the complex layers of Metallica's music, and as such was so much more able to connect to his intended audience. We should also realize that, now approaching his thirties, any more songs about blood death and destruction were kinda old hat, and those Metallica songs that were written in that style were written by aggressive young metal kids for other like-minded aggressive young metal kids.

Throughout "Through The Never" we can hear Hetfield in contemplative mood musing upon questions that have occurred to all of us at one time or another: Who am I? What am I doing here? Is there anyone else "out there" in this vast blackness of space? Here there are no tales of death to be found, just more questions to be asked.

It is significant to note that, on first inspection at least, Hetfield's point of view takes no account of any spiritual need; there is almost no religious perspective to be found at all as he assesses this planet Earth he coldly refers to as, "Our home, third stone from the sun". Yet very mention of the word "heavens" in the strikingly poetic line, "Gazing up to the breeze of the heavens" and it's almost as if Hetfield is yearning for a sign that there might be a God after all. But having exposed this vulnerable need James then crushes that hope under a wealth of nihilistic maths. Adopting an appreciation of the world's physical state in the universe that is almost physics textbook stuff, he surmises that we're locked on a planet that is tumbling through space with no place to

go. You very much get the feeling that there are unresolved spiritual issues kicking around Hetfield's soul that are doing battle between a hope for redemption and his rational mind's bleak atheism.

It's also quite possible to believe that James is having a sly laugh at the human condition inasmuch as we all know what the physical facts of our place in the universe entail (maybe James had just finished reading Stephen Hawking's *A Brief History Of Time*?), yet we are tortured by not having any of our spiritual beliefs proven. It's as if James is suggesting that humanity is part of some huge cosmic-wide joke, and we've failed to appreciate that in fact it is our lonely, random existence that is the punch line.

Whatever the actual case, it's pretty obvious that at no point prior to this have we ever seen a more intimate or philosophical set of lyrics from the man Hetfield.

Nothing Else Matters

'The word "harmonies" has never been a bad word in the Metallica camp'

James Hetfield, Rolling Stone, 1991

When "Nothing Else Matters" first hit the airwaves there were two distinct reactions. The first was utter horror from the Metalli-army faithful – beyond all doubt, this was a Metallica sold down the river. The second was one of joy and relief. It was a joy to hear Hetfield finally letting the melody in his singing voice breathe, and a relief to think that there was now something accessible enough for the rest of the world to get its ears around without being terrified of the name Metallica. You can't please both perspectives at the same time and, frankly,

The T-shirt says it all: do not mess with this band.

Metallica pandered to neither as they concentrated on taking the song's natural harmonies to their maximum potential.

"Nothing Else Matters" wasn't just a ballad, it was a ballad with heartfelt, genuine lyrics and a full-blown orchestra to boot – if Metallica were gonna sell out then, dammit, they were gonna sell out in style!

Lyrically, though, "Nothing Else Matters" was far from your typical "I've lost you baby, and my heart is bleeding" drivel that so many of the late Eighties/early Nineties rock acts were forced to write in order to appeal to the female vote. Acts such as Kiss ("Forever"), Def Leppard ("Hysteria"/"Love Bites") Bon Jovi ("Living In Sin" et al), Poison ("Every Rose Has Its Thorn"), White Lion ("When The Children Cry"), GN'R ("Don't Cry"/"November Rain") and even metal hellraisers Mötley Crüe ("Without You") had all churned out sentimental, over-produced crap, born out of a sheer desperation to hike at least some semblance of their music onto radio. But since Metallica had already become a huge-selling act without the need for radio airplay, their decision to record "Nothing Else Matters" could hardly have been based on breaking into any lucrative AOR markets. Lyrically too "Nothing Else Matters" was quite apart from any of the saccharine sweet ballads that other acts had released, there were no lost laments and "I still love you baby"'s here, as James's song was a more open and honest soul-laid-bare appeal to like-minded people wherever they may be.

If tearful teens wished to hear James's line: "Couldn't be much more from the heart/Forever trusting who we are", as one lover speaking to another, then fine, but as the song builds it becomes much more the sound of man taking on the uncomfortable task of exposing his inner feelings in order to bond with his friends. James could be speaking to mythical comrades in arms, maybe even his literal comrades in Metallica, or again, it could be another moment of reflection and appreciation for the army of Metallica fans that the band found themselves playing to on the two-year-long "Damaged Justice" tour when the song was written.

The song was sweet enough to ensnare the middle ground, yet still tough enough to get all but the hardcore

James sings from the heart.

misty-eyed at the thought of the shared sacrifice – "Life is ours, we live it our way" being the key line in that reading.

James admitted to the *Providence Journal Bulletin* that he had written "Nothing Else Matters" in a moment of vulnerability while on the road in Canada at the tail end of their 275-date trek in 1990, saying, "I wrote it when I was lonely" (2.165). Speaking in 1991, Lars considered that much of the tone of James's lyrics for this new album had come from within, as part of a maturing process that they had all been through, commenting, "...the songs are a result of what's been lingering in James. You can look around for the things that make you feel mad and you write about them. This time it's been a matter of looking within, the experiences that you've been through" (1.53).

Talking about the accessible nature of the song in '91, James added that the band wanted, "...a song that wasn't your typical Metallica ballad...We wanted to build it a little more vocally. I think that the string arrangement on it is pretty fucking cool. If we're going to go for this kind of song we might as well go the whole way" (1.47).

Of Wolf and Man

It's been argued that James came up with "Of Wolf and Man" because he'd already been nicknamed "wolfman" due to his long mane of hair and encroaching facial sideburns, but it's probably just a laughable coincidence. Caught on tape in '92 James admitted, "I like the animalistic part of man and nature. I don't know, sometimes I look around and see all the crap that we've accumulated. I mean, what the fuck do we need all this shit for anyway? 'Of Wolf And Man' essentially brings things back to the basics, back to the meaning of life. The song illustrates the similarities between wolves and men, and there are similarities" (1.53).

At the end of the marathon "Damaged Justice" tour, James was searching for an escape. A heavy recreational drinker, James reasoned that now off tour

he needed a hobby if he was to preserve any real sanity. A reunion with his estranged father, a keen hunter, led James to take up the activity as a distraction to the clutter and noise in his regular life. Pretty soon Hetfield was taking regular trips to the wilderness alongside fellow wild man of rock Ted Nugent, a vehement anti-drink and drugs campaigner and advocate of the wilderness' all-cleansing spirit. "Of Wolf and Man", then, is almost certainly Hetfield's take on the thrill of the hunt and his desire for a more simple, basic life.

As a harking back to old Metallica the song builds almost identically to "Creeping Death", with which it shares a kindred spirit – stalking, silent, death creeping through the night. Unlike any other lyrics on the record ("Enter Sandman" notwithstanding) "Of Wolf..." is also a clear throwback to the old *Ride the Lightning* lyric style too – a fantasy "what if?" perspective in which the scenario being presented is "imagine if you were a werewolf."

Preposterous as it may seem given the more introspective lyrics on the rest of the decidedly mature "black" album, "Of Wolf..." is nevertheless outstanding fun to listen to and howl along with at a huge rock gig! It also shows that despite their assertions to having grown up, Metallica were still capable of having a laugh while James was able to put a very primal point across – Metallica still have teeth.

Indeed, despite the media games and re-interpretations that were to follow with the confused *Load/Reload* eras, Metallica were always the "monsters" in the US rock scene. Nine Inch Nails, Soundgarden, Pearl Jam and that whole early Nineties Lollapalooza counter-culture scene were never truly accepting of Metallica's musical raison d'être of aggression for aggression's sake, and they viewed it as somehow unnecessary, vulgar or, worse still, juvenile.

When Metallica accepted the headline slot at the very last Lollapalooza trek in 1995, maybe James should have screamed out the lyrics to "Of Wolf..." just that little bit louder, so that the ever-media-savvy Lars, who had insisted that the band should begin to expose themselves to a different, more "alternative" crowd, could have heard him over the incessant chattering of the sycophants.

The God That Failed

"'The God that Failed' is a very personal song for James. It's about this mind-washing Christian Science stuff, where people think that they can go around medicine and be healed of their ills. I know some people will say, "The God That Failed", isn't that about Satan?' Well, no, it's not about that at all" (1.43).

If ever James Hetfield was heading toward a lyric he had been dreading to write, then this song had to be the one. For although "The God That Failed" was his direct attack upon the Christian Scientist movement *per se*, it's a song that also reflects the deep-rooted centre of his own angers and fears.

James Hetfield's mother had died of cancer when he was only 17. James believed that had she not been a lifelong Christian Scientist, and had she accepted traditional medical treatment, his mother would have beaten the cancer and she would still have been alive today. The lines "It feeds/It grows/It clouds all that you will know" speak not only about the brainwashing doctrine of blind faith, but also the physical spread of unchecked cancer.

You have to wonder whether the deeply cynical world-view that the young James Hetfield had recounted through the eyes of his many song characters is a reflection of the deep hurt and bleak nihilism that any young man might be compelled to construct around him, having witnessed his mother believe in the healing power of a God that may not even exist. To believe that a supernatural being will save you when medical technology is right at hand seems irresponsible as much as it does misguided.

Hetfield's cutting lines, "Trust you gave/A child to save/Left you cold and him in a grave", could well be about a specific incident that a young Hetfield was recounting, as, like all children of Christian Scientists, James was subjected to many Sunday social gatherings with other offspring. It could also be a metaphysical remark about himself, inasmuch as it might well have felt like the death of his own childhood when James's mother died.

There is much bitterness, loathing and resentment within the lines, "Pride you took/Pride you feel/Pride that you felt when you'd kneel", as James spits yet more hatred at the self-serving nature that lies at the heart of many western religions. In essence, James is saying, "You would keep your only child away from medical cures in order to prove to yourself that you love God more than the next person."

Anyone unconvinced of the "cynical voice" behind the song "Through The Never" might do well to read the lyrics to "The God That Failed", and remember that James's early life experiences had moulded his inner emotional defences into castle walls.

It took Bob Rock weeks of persuasion with the stripping away of these various barriers, via the art of gentle encouragement, to create an atmosphere possible for Hetfield to broach this darkest of personal subjects. Bob, like everyone else, wanted to understand from where all the pent-up rage and anger within James and his often mean-spirited, death-obsessed lyrics were coming from. In the end, reasoned James, it would have been a shame to have not taken advantage of the new-found openness that was bouncing around the San Francisco-based rehearsal room.

When reading the lyrics to the song you get the impression that Hetfield is holding nothing back. Much noise was made in the media when Korn and another rather death-obsessed singer, Jonathan Davis, arrived on the metal scene in '94. Critics argued that Korn producer Ross Robinson had encouraged the performance of a lifetime out of the troubled young man who was practically having a nervous breakdown as he recorded the vocals to "Faget". Raw, stirring stuff though Korn's debut undoubtedly is, for this writer's money, if you want stinging, primal honesty, where you can look directly into the soul of a songwriter, then you still need look no further than "The God That Failed".

It would have been easy, one suspects, for Metallica to convince themselves that such a touchy subject required yet another melancholic musical approach like the one on "The Unforgiven". Wisely they adopted a more proactive approach as James delivers venom-laced lyric

after lyric, while the stabbing riffs shoot holes through the supposed "truth" of blind optimism.

My Friend Misery

'This song is about people who take their responsibility on their shoulders but find out the people they think they represent aren't really behind them at all.'

Lars Ulrich, 1991

Being the first song that Jason Newsted had been allowed to develop with the band since he joined in 1986, you'd be forgiven for expecting a little more bass-led action than is in evidence on record. Still, when James Hetfield is on a rant then he sure lets you know. We can pity the poor bastard who ended up on the end of this particular tirade (one of the give-peace-a-chance brigade who were hanging him out to dry over "Don't Tread On Me", perhaps?).

Though the song's specific intended target will no doubt remain lost to the realms of whichever beer-fuelled rant first instigated it, the themes behind the song are familiar to us all. How many times have you sat in front of a TV and heard a politician, or worse still, a "concerned campaigner" speak of issues that "deeply affect us all" only for you to look around and think, "You mean issues that specifically affect you and yours, not me and mine"?

If you were to add "concerned rock stars" to the list of activists with a supposed 'something to say', then we might be getting closer still to the actual root of the song. It's entirely feasible James endured hearing some rant from a save-the-rainforest or feed-the-Third-World type and either considered the person saying it was misusing the public platform they'd been given as a musician or, more than likely, didn't have the first damn clue what they were talking about anyway! As the 1990s progressed, innumerable conscience-led rock stars, most notably from the suburbs of Seattle, would go on to bore the pants off an utterly disinterested generation of MTV-bred teens.

Ultimately, "My Friend Misery" provokes questions back at the song's accused, challenging them to look around and see anyone else who cares as much as they do. It asks, "Do you know what you're even fighting for or are you just making all this noise just because you can?"

Like "The God That Failed", then, "My Friend Misery" is another attack on the false superiority of the deluded self-righteous – only, unlike the former, it's actually quite light-hearted (albeit in a sneering manner).

The Struggle Within

It's tempting to speculate that a great number of the lyrical voices contained within Metallica are speaking from James's internalized perspective. The whole band went on record to say that they all understood that the lyrics were way more personal for the record than at any other time in the band's ten-year career, and Hetfield himself has long been reticent to explain his thoughts behind the songs, leaving either Lars to fill in the blanks or preferring the fans to draw their own conclusions from his comments. So when approaching 'The Struggle Within' it is all too tempting to assume that James must so obviously be struggling with some raging inner demon again, and has come up with a song about self-hatred.

Well, perhaps he did, but like most good lyricists James is hardly confined to a self-centred point of view when it comes to expressing his inner thoughts. Believing that a song always shows the inner

machinations of how a lyricist thinks, particularly one as private as James Hetfield, is always going to be a rewarding process, no matter if it's accurate or not. The pay-off comes in the time you put in rather than the truth of the matter, because at least then you have engaged with the dialogue on a level above that of simply repeating the words in the manner of some meaningless mantra. As Lars remarks on the intro page to this book, "Like a lot of what James writes, even if you have the lyrics right in front of you, there's still so many possibilities in there. That's the greatest thing about his lyrics."

With that in mind, then, "The Struggle Within" can be taken in many different ways. It is entirely possible that Hetfield is focussing upon an aspect of his own personality that he finds fault with, and is attempting to set it down on paper in a moment of exorcism. Alternatively – and for my money, more probably – this is James once again focussing on a negative characteristic that he sees in certain other people – or maybe even a weakness in the human spirit in general. By highlighting the weakness, he is first of all encouraging us all to take stock of our weak points and then perhaps to do something about them.

It should be pretty obvious by now that Hetfield hates whingers, moaners and whiners – songs such as "Sad But True", "The Unforgiven" and "Holier Than Thou" all deal with negative mental viewpoints that, in turn, have a larger impact in the real world. Hetfield, like most of his conservative male audience, is more naturally aligned to the typically strong, defiant, macho credo advocated in "Don't Tread On Me", "Wherever I May Roam" and "Of Wolf And Man". Though on the later *Load/Reload* records James's black/white, right/wrong, sure-as-shit world-view takes a self-imposed beating (perhaps partly due to the impending responsibilities of fatherhood), with the *Metallica*-era material we can probably put these values down to him being hugely successful while still a relatively young man, when everything he says publicly is generally reinforced by the return in gold and platinum discs. With that sort of life, it's not too hard to believe that the world doesn't work the way you think it does.

Happy Days: Album sales were racking up around the world.

7

Load

Reload

'I certainly didn't expect *Load* to be as successful as *Metallica*. Timing has something to do with everything that goes on. If you look at what was happening in '91 with us and Guns N' Roses, before Nirvana, before Pearl Jam, it was the right thing at the right time. If the "black album" (*Metallica*) came out tomorrow, I don't think it'd do twenty million copies.'

Lars Ulrich, 1997 (1:100)

'We put out an album (*Metallica*) and suddenly we were surrounded by the mainstream. With this album we're back out at the edges. James put it very succinctly. He said, "We're being hated again and I kinda like it." I can totally relate to that.'

Kirk Hammett, 1996 (1:100)

In the five years between *Metallica*, aka the "black album", and *Load*, Metallica kept up a punishing live schedule, virtually living on the road between 1991 and 1994, but all the while continuing to write, amassing a large body of songs that would form the meat of the next project. Some songs were demoed at Lars Ulrich's house in mid-1994 – including one called "Load", though it would appear on the album as "King Nothing". In February of 1995 they entered The Plant in Sausolito, California with Bob Rock, to start work on what was originally intended to be a double album that would be 27 songs long. Apart from a summer break during

which they played four dates, the so-called "Escape From the Studio" tour – including a headlining spot at Castle Donington where they previewed two songs from the album, "2x4" and "Devil's Dance" – they remained there until December, though according to Lars, they had finished recording all the songs by the middle of the summer. They just needed to be mixed and otherwise polished for release.

When the band were offered a slot on the Lollapalooza tour (along with Soundgarden, Devo and The Ramones) they took the decision to hold off on completing the record. According to Lars: "We said okay, instead of finishing all this material and making it a double album, why don't we just divide it into two different records, put one out in the summer, go and play Lollapalooza, have a quick nip around the world, go in and finish the songs and put another record out next year?" (*Metal Hammer*, December '97, p 49).

There was a precedent for bands doing this, most notably their rivals Guns N' Roses, who released *Use Your Illusion* in two parts.

But there were other reasons for splitting the album, reasons that were to do with tensions in the band that arose from the constant touring: "Another reason that we wanted to split the records up is that we wanted to get away from the trap we felt stuck in, which was that we would put out these records and then go on these never-ending tours. What we wanted to try to do, to save Metallica and continue Metallica for a long time, was try and make more records more often and less touring less often" (ibid, p 51).

They were the biggest metal band in the world: it could have been a big temptation for them to remain so by retreading the formula that they had perfected on *Metallica*. But in the time since that album, the world had changed. The divisions between what was "heavy metal" and what was "alternative rock" had dissolved in the wake of Jane's Addiction, Pearl Jam and particularly Nirvana. By the mid-1990s, seemingly disparate forms of music – metal, hip-hop, techno, pop, jazz, blues – were being broken down and put back together in new ways. Bands like Rage Against The Machine, Nine Inch Nails and particularly Korn, whose breakthrough album came after *Metallica* was released, were forging a new metal sound and redefining the metal aesthetic. In many ways Metallica represented the end of one particular line of hard rock's evolution; they were all astute enough to see that the next record had to be the beginning of something else.

It was clear that they were reaching out beyond the confines of the genre of music that they had done so much to define. Before they even set foot in the studio there were some intriguing hints as to what the album might be like: at the 1995 MTV Music Awards, rap mogul Dr Dre was told by an MTV reporter that Metallica wanted to work with him. "Well I don't wanna work with them," said a taciturn Dre. Lars made his affection for Britpop sensations Oasis and Black Grape known, even approaching Oasis with a view to going on tour with Metallica. "Oasis have got the best singer, they're the biggest band in the world and they've sold more albums than anybody else, except for us," he told MTV in 1996. Unlikely bedfellows indeed. His cover version of "Wonderwall" – performed on the 1997 Lollapalooza tour – is still something of an embarrassment that can silence a room full of Metallica fans.

And there were to be remixes: German industrial band Die Krupps had already reworked some Metallica songs that had resulted in James throwing the stereo that they were playing on against the wall. This time around they approached New York vegetarian techno-DJ Moby to rework the first single from the album, "Until It Sleeps". The results had them smashing the stereo again, though they went ahead and released it anyway.

And it wasn't only the new musical direction that rubbed hardcore fans up the wrong way: gone was the Metallica logo, replaced by what looked like a half-assed compromise between something new and the old one. And the band were no longer the men in black...unless you count eyeliner.

It didn't even look like a metal record. The album arrived packaged in a sleeve featuring a piece of art by infamous New York-based artist Andres Serrano: the "painting" is called *Blood and Semen III* and was made by mixing bovine blood and the artist's semen and pressing it under plexiglass. Kirk discovered the picture in a collection of Serrano's works at a bookstore. The accompanying photographs by Anton Corbijn, a photographer whose arty monochrome imagery is mainly associated with Joy Division, U2 and Depeche Mode, depicted the band sitting around a table, the colours washed out, almost sepia like an old photograph. Lars is smoking a cigar, everyone looks moody, wearing shades with short hair dressed in suits, proving that there was more in their wardrobe than black cap-sleeved T-shirts and black drainpipe jeans.

Times have changed: Hetfield's stage presence has transformed dramatically over the years.

Load (1996)
Ain't my Bitch

Any fears that they were about to produce an art-rock album, or a rap-rock album or – God forbid – a sort of alt.rock Britpop album, were allayed by the opening tracks, which harked back to the 1970s, to greasy blue-collar head-out-on-the-highway biker rock. James Hetfield's transition as a lyricist and songwriter from a callow youth who spoke through his characters in apocalyptic science fantasy scenarios to a mature man turning his gaze firmly on his own heart and soul was complete. The songs on *Load* are all about James, about his anger, his pain, his loss and not about a second or third person standing in for him. The songs are full of the same bitterness, but there is a more contemplative side to *Load* and *Reload* in which he is trying to find the roots of the anger and to deal with the causes. The album's opener, "Ain't My Bitch", is an aggressive statement of rejection. His "bitch" may be a person, female or otherwise, whom he feels is invading his life. "You arrived, but now it's time to kiss your ass goodbye/Dragging me down." It could also be about a problem that somebody expects him to resolve.

An intriguing alternative interpretation is suggested by Hetfield's decision in 2003 to seek treatment for his alcoholism and "other addictions"; the "bitch" that's "dragging [him] down" may be the substances that constantly surround touring bands. The tone of the song is slightly ambiguous: Hetfield is asking the question: "Why you around?" Yet this doesn't quite sit with the absolute rejection of the opening verse. Is this temptation speaking? The track sets the tone for the "new" Metallica sound, right down to Kirk Hammett's slide guitar solo adding a bluesy, almost Southern-boogie feel to the song, something that was to be explored on other songs on *Load* and *Reload* and would prepare fans for their "country" song "Mama Said" later on the album, or their cover version of Bob Seger's "Turn the Page" in 1998.

*Style over content? Many **Load** fans balked at the band's makeover.*

2X4

Another deep bluesy boogie track with more than a whiff of ZZ Top, Creedence Clearwater Revival or Lynyrd Skynyrd about it, it's also one of the most aggressive, most negative songs on the record. "'2X4' was the first riff written for the album – it came from way back; I remember soundchecks goofing around on that riff," said Hetfield (*Guitar Player* magazine, November 1996). The title refers to a plank of wood, sometimes called a "Belfast sleeping pill": an object that you would use to batter somebody with, but also in a metaphorical sense it's about being unable to communicate with somebody because it's like trying to talk to a piece of wood: "I'm gonna make you, shake you, take you/I'm gonna be that one who breaks you."

Publicity shots from the Load/Reload *era became what can generously be described as a "slight departure" from traditional metal.*

Then "Make my day" – the line lifted from *Dirty Harry* now officially the favoured come-on challenge of small town bar-brawlers and wife-beaters everywhere – and "are you talking to me?" from *Taxi Driver* recur throughout the song. It's about violence as catharsis, the energy of anger and hate. It could be an interrogation, a torture scene: it could also be about the frustration of trying to communicate.

"The song '2X4' took on the feet of, uh, smashing someone with a piece of wood, y'know? Instead of trying to out-think someone, just out-smash 'em. Hatred is a big part of my life, and has been for a long while. It's easier to find something to hate than something to like" (1:101).

The House That Jack Built

One of the heaviest, almost psychedelic tracks on the album – the rather odd guitar solo is a voice box (as made famous by Peter Frampton on "Show Me The Way") played through a wah-wah pedal – "The House That Jack Built" is probably the most blatant statement about drugs and addiction that Hetfield has ever made. It may not actually be his own experience, even though he sings from a first-person point of view. The title could refer to heroin – to "jack up" being junkie parlance for injecting the narcotic – though it is scarcely a pro-drug song. James takes the role of addict as seeker: "Open door so I walk inside/Swallow me so the pain subsides". But any insights or escapes he gains come at a very high and bitter price.

"The House That Jack Built" follows in a long tradition of anti-drug songs, such as "Sister Morphine" (co-written by Mick Jagger and Marianne Faithfull – she would appear as a guest vocalist on "The Memory Remains" on *Reload*) and Black Sabbath's "Snowblind".

"The House That Jack Built" is cited by many fans as the first signs of a "crack" in the album, one of the weakest songs that the band had recorded. Many hardcore thrash fans regarded the entire album as a kind of betrayal, referring to the band snidely as "Alternica", implying that they had "sold out" for a more lucrative or "respectable" alt.rock crowd.

Until it Sleeps

The first single release from *Load* and, based on singles sales, Metallica's fifth largest hit to date. A smouldering, angry ballad; like "Dyer's Eve" and "The God That Failed" it was influenced by Hetfield's Christian Science upbringing, this time it specifically deals with the subject of his father Virgil's painful, unmedicated death from cancer, just like his mother's. It's a rage against a God who let both his parents die believing themselves to be flawed for having insufficient faith to cure themselves. It's a rage against the unfairness of it all, the randomness with which the disease strikes: "So tell me why you've chosen me/Don't want your grip/Don't want your greed"

There are signs that hint at other meanings in the song too: in the video for the single, which was directed by Samuel Bayer and inspired by the famous Hieronymus Bosch painting *The Garden Of Earthly Delights*, the figure of Christ bears an uncanny resemblance to Cliff Burton.

Odd, then, that such a dark song would prove to be such a big commercial success in the glossy MTV world.

"Until It Sleeps" was written in the studio while the band were jamming around on the riff: without anyone being aware of it, producer Bob Rock pressed "Record" and captured the raw essence of what the single would become. It was originally called "F.O.B.D.", which stands for "Fell On Black Days".

King Nothing

Originally entitled "Load", "King Nothing" is the most consciously "old school" song on the album: it would not have been out of place on *Ride the Lightning* and as such remains one of the most popular cuts on this album even by fans who disliked the rest of it. It's a straightforward song about thwarted ambition, avarice and cosmic justice, playing on lines from nursery rhymes: "I want the star/I want it now/I want it all and I don't care how." The song is perhaps inspired by the myth of King Midas – the mythical man who was granted the power to turn everything he touched to gold. He went around his palace changing everything into gold. After a while, he started to get hungry and thirsty, but his "blessing" turned everything to gold, and this included everything he tried to eat or drink. It is the origin of the moral: "Be careful what you wish for, you just might get it", which is repeated in the song's bridge. Whether this is James expressing regret at some personal Faustian pact, or at the desperate avarice he saw around him in the music industry, is anybody's guess.

Hero of the Day

Metallica called the track's demo "Mouldy" because its riff had been around for a very long time before they turned it into a song. If there was one song that was singled out by the purists as an example of the "new" Metallica's

Dressed down to kill.

heresy it was this one, and it's not hard to see why. "Hero Of The Day" could have been an REM song or an Alice In Chains song; if you played it blind to somebody there's very little chance that Metallica would be their first guess. It starts as a ballad with an ascending bass and guitar riff, with James singing "clean", building to a powerful crescendo with a string section underscoring the REM comparisons.

The dilemma of any band changing a winning formula – whether it is a pop band trying to make serious rock or a serious rock band like Metallica trying to spread their wings – is that the original supporters will feel alienated, and "Hero Of The Day", while garnering good critical reviews in the mainstream press, upset a lot of the "true believers". Fears that Metallica were turning their backs on metal were underscored by interviews given at the time of the album's release. Kirk Hammett said: "We were a heavy metal band seven or eight years ago. I think we started our separation some time around the 'black' album. We definitely have our roots in heavy metal, but I think we're much more than a heavy metal band... We haven't outgrown or turned our back on anything. We're just so much more than that." Ironically, the song is about the dark side of hero-worship, about the unconditional love of a parent for children who have gone off to follow "the hero of the day" and their fear that this hero will turn out to be malign. And heroes will always let you down.

Bleeding Me

Another slow-building Metallica power-ballad, if "Hero Of The Day" was the song that got them sneeringly referred to as "Altallica"' then "Bleeding Me" was the one that restored the faith of some of those same fans. A dark and moody song with an edgy slow-motion riff and a sinister organ lurking in the background, adding a touch of Doors-like gothic menace, the song is about ambition and how the things that hold us back and torture us are all of our own making: "This thorn in my side is from the tree/This thorn in my side is from the tree I've

planted". Again it's tempting to interpret all of Hetfield's lyrics in the light of his subsequent admission of drink problems, though while the lyrics on *Load* and *Reload* are more personal, they aren't necessarily confessional. Nevertheless, both "Bleeding Me" and the song that follows it on the album – "Cure" – could be interpreted as his feelings of powerlessness in the face of a failing – alcoholism – that is, both within and oustide his control at the same time.

"Around the time of *Load*, I felt I wanted to stop drinking," Hetfield said. "Maybe I'm missing out something. Everyone else seems so happy all the time. I want to get happy. I'd plan my life around a hangover: 'The Misfits are playing in town Friday night, so Saturday is hangover day.' I lost a lot of days in my life. Going to therapy for a year, I learned a lot about

myself. There's a lot of things that scare you when you're growing up, you don't know why. The song 'Bleeding Me' is about that: I was trying to bleed out all bad, get the evil out. While I was going through therapy, I discovered some ugly stuff in there. A dark spot." (*Playboy*, April 2001: 125).

As an example of the new, more personal style of songwriting, "Bleeding Me" is one of the highlights of *Load*, the most successful attempt by Metallica to do something new while hanging on to their roots as the all-time great thrash band.

Cure

Another bluesy, hard-riff driven song, not exactly one of their most memorable songs, being neither instant nor a song that grows with repeated listenings. But it's prime Metallica at their angriest. This is a song about alcoholism, self-destruction, addiction and cures often being worse than the disease. It begins with the image of a man drinking: "He takes his medicine/The man takes another bullet".

A "bullet" refers to a can of Coors Lite, Hetfield's favourite brew, which is known as a Silver Bullet. But just as he has been deluded into thinking that drink is the answer to his problems, we switch to an image of somebody embracing religion. The dilemma is that everyone deals with their own insecurities with different "cures" – booze, drugs, religion – that only work for you so long as you "believe". Again, while it may be a personal song, James may not actually be writing about himself but about a more general culture of crutches that people rely on to get them through the day.

Poor Twisted Me

Although it's a parody of bombastic Seventies blues-rock like, for example, Whitesnake's 'Mistreated', (the riff is almost a straight lift from Canned Heat's 'On The Road Again') this is one of the best hard rockers on *Load*. According to Hetfield: "'Poor Twisted Me' is ZZ Top, right there. That riff just came out of fucking around in Lars' dungeon. I was goofing with an echo setting, and that set the timing for that song. And then we came in and put a beat to it and it had a pretty kinda greasy groove to it." (*Guitar Player* magazine, November 1996).

Like "My Friend Of Misery" on the "black" album, the album also sends up the woe-is-me complaint rock popular with adolescents then as now: written in the wake of Kurt Cobain's suicide, the first Korn album and countless misunderstood little flowers full of issues concerning mom and pop, it is about people who love to

tell you about the pain they're in: "Good to feel my friend/Oh woe is me". It also inspired the "Poor Touring Me" and "Re-Touring Me" shows.

Wasting my Hate

The connections between country and metal are few and tenuous, so the fact that this song was actually inspired by a story that "outlaw" country star Waylon Jennings told to James is one of those rare links. Jennings was sitting in a diner, and noticed a man outside in a car staring at him, giving him the "evil eye". So Waylon stared back with hate, and finally lost his temper and went out to talk to the guy in the car, only to find out that he was sleeping, and it was in fact the light reflecting on the windscreen that made it look as though he was staring. Jennings thought, "Oh man, I've wasted my hate on this guy." James was teamed up with Jennings by a college radio station who wanted one outlaw to interview another: James took along some Waylon Jennings CDs to be autographed for his dad, while Jennings presented him with some Metallica albums that he wanted autographed for his son. The two hit it off in an unlikely friendship, with Hetfield later contributing a cover of "Don't You Think This Outlaw Bit's Done Got Out of Hand" for a tribute album in 2003. The song, according to James, is actually inspired as much by his father as by Jennings. It's a pugnacious song, a song about rising above provocation: "Ain't gonna waste my hate/But I'm so greedy when they say."

Mama Said

The most talked about and probably the most hated or loved or misunderstood song that Metallica have ever recorded. If "Nothing Else Matters" was seen by some

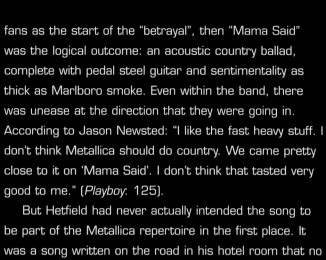

fans as the start of the "betrayal", then "Mama Said" was the logical outcome: an acoustic country ballad, complete with pedal steel guitar and sentimentality as thick as Marlboro smoke. Even within the band, there was unease at the direction that they were going in. According to Jason Newsted: "I like the fast heavy stuff. I don't think Metallica should do country. We came pretty close to it on 'Mama Said'. I don't think that tasted very good to me." (*Playboy*: 125).

But Hetfield had never actually intended the song to be part of the Metallica repertoire in the first place. It was a song written on the road in his hotel room that no one was supposed to hear. It was personal, for him alone. He wrote it on an electric guitar, but always envisioned it as an acoustic song at the time when he was big on country, particularly Waylon Jennings, Johnny Cash and Hank Williams. He had originally been thinking that he could sell it or collaborate with someone as part of a solo project.

He wrote the song about his mother, pouring into it all his feelings of regret at the way he had distanced himself from her while she was alive: "Rebel my new last name/Wild blood in my veins."

There's a long tradition in country songs of hard men and gunfighters asking forgiveness, and beer-soaked sentimentality is often the flipside of macho bravado. It's not only the "straightest" song that Metallica have ever recorded, but also the most plainly autobiographical song that Hetfield has written. It also opened up a lot of new areas for Metallica, such as their "unplugged" set at Neil Young's annual Bridge School Benefit in 1997 alongside Alanis Morissette, Blues Traveller, Dave Matthews and Smashing Pumpkins. Fears that Metallica were joining the mainstream were not without foundation.

James screams for Mama.

Thorn Within

Another slice of old school pitch-black Metallica heaviness, as though to prove that they were still capable of turning them out. Had the entire album been made up of songs like this, the hardcore fans would have been delighted. It's another stab at religion, awash in Christian imagery ("Forgive me father/For I have sinned" from the Roman Catholic confessional, the "thorn within" from the crown of thorns, the "mark of shame" from the mark of Cain) and the way it manipulates people into feeling that they are unworthy.

This song is, it seems, evidently about a search for forgiveness for some guilt, real or imagined, that the song's protagonist knows he will never find, in some ways a continuation of some of the themes from "Mama Said". It could also be about a resentful Cain or Christ figure, condemned to bear the burden for all of humanity's sins. According to Jason Newsted, the song is his favourite on the whole album, though strangely for such a vintage Metallica song, they have never actually played it live.

Ronnie

The AC/DC-like penultimate song on the album was inspired by a high school shooting in Washington State in the early Nineties by a kid named "Ron Brown" ("Ronnie Frown" in the song), though possibly the "real" case was that of Barry Loukaitis, a 14-year-old who dressed up like a gunslinger with two concealed pistols, 78 rounds of ammunition and a high-powered rifle. He shot three people and blamed "mood swings". Loukaitis had thought it would be "fun" to go on a killing spree, was convicted of two counts of aggravated first-degree murder and sentenced to two mandatory life terms without parole. In the wake of the Columbine school shootings in 1999, media pundits actually attempted to draw some connection between this song and the so-called "trench coat mafia". The characters in songs like 'Harvester Of Sorrow' are drawn from comics and slasher movies; "Ronnie Frown" is from CNN, though Hetfield treats the whole thing as a piece of very black comedy: "Now we all know why children called him Ronnie Frown/When he pulled that gun from his pocket/They'd all fall down".

The Outlaw Torn

In the lead-up to the release of *Load*, Lars Ulrich dropped the suggestion that "The Outlaw Torn" may in fact be the greatest heavy metal song ever written. Weighing in at ten minutes, it's obvious that they intended this to be one of those weighty classics that can only be followed by silence. Good as it is, it isn't even the best Metallica song ever written, though it is the most memorable track from *Load*, not least for the barely restrained guitar interplay with Kirk and James swapping around lead and rhythm roles and for the loose, jam-like structure of the piece that seems to stretch on and on, with the guitar duel building to a climax. The song is about losing somebody and waiting desperately for somebody to come and take their place, though they never do. Like much of the writing on *Load*, it is about James coming to terms with the loss of his mother and his father's illness, and it's about how nobody can replace the understanding that they gave to him: "And if I close my mind in fear/Please pry it open."

The original take had to be edited by around half a minute so that it would fit on to the CD – which, at over 78 minutes, was already at bursting point – and it seems to finish rather abruptly. That *Load* was such a chunk of music to digest all at one sitting, one wonders how the listener would have fared had the band actually gone ahead and made a double album with the further 13 songs that would appear a year later on *Reload*.

Reload (1997)

'If you record a double album it only counts as one on your contract, whereas this way it counts as two... we get to the pot of gold at the end even quicker!'

Lars Ulrich, 1997 (1:102)

'There's stuff on this album that's as classic as Led Zeppelin and Black Sabbath. That's the thing with Metallica. It's not just a project for me. It's the chance to work with a band I consider to be the new Led Zeppelin or The Beatles. They're pretty much the Bob Dylan of this generation. Let's face facts – it's not Mötley Crüe who are gonna go down in the history books...'

Bob Rock, 1997 (1: 102)

Metallica the unstoppable style machine roll on.

With *Load* having sold almost precisely half of what the 'black album' sold, it was hardly a commercial disaster, though major labels are known to become nervous if an artist brings in a profit that's smaller than the profits that they generated in the past. Still, the band went back into the studio after touring to complete the project that they had set themselves. Initially there were conflicting reports as to what people could expect on the second part of the package: "We've started to listen to a lot of very different types of music. I got heavily into blues and jazz. Bringing in all these influences definitely changes all our ways of thinking, and that's basically why *Reload* sounds so different... we're different people now," said Kirk (1:102), dropping hints that his listening taste was no longer Mercyful Fate but jazz giants Miles Davis, John Coltrane and Art Pepper. The first single from *Load*, "Until It Sleeps", was remixed by New York techno-DJ Moby, an unsatisfying exercise for all concerned. "There was a German group (Die Krupps) that did some of our songs and the first time I heard it I was shocked. But there was a certain unnamed member of this group who, when he heard what they had done, made the CD player travel into the wall," said Lars (1: 100). "We ended up giving this track ('Until It Sleeps') to Moby... but this time we threw it at the wall and kept it."

"It's more [one-dimensional than *Load*], it'll be 10 or 12 five-minute songs that are all fairly heavy. No 10-minute epics, or James going off on his country tangent," said Lars, as though to assuage the fears of Metallica fans that they could expect an album of be-bop, folk and techno experiments (1:102). The resulting album in fact contained just as many "country tangents" as *Load*, though it contained just as many straight-ahead blues-tinged hard rock songs as well. Some jaundiced fans have debated whether it is possible that you can build one great Metallica album from *Load* and *Reload*. However, it wasn't necessarily the music that worried fans.

The band were annoyed that so much of the attention from disgruntled fans and the media had focussed on their new image – the suits, the short hair, the bad make-up, Kirk's increasingly lurid "pimp" clothes – as much as on the music itself. Reviews in heavyweight mainstream publications like *Rolling Stone* and *Spin* were

Load/Reload

Kirk checks out his reflection and a Cuban pimp-meister stares back.

however: when they visited the UK to appear at the Reading Festival, he told one music paper that *Reload* would sound like The Spice Girls. This throwaway remark was picked up by websites and earnestly debated by Metallica fans, convinced the "sell-out" was now complete.

"When you put us next to Sepultura or something like that, I know we're so much old men, but there's one thing I can tell you, it's that live, we can fucking wipe the floor with any of these bands. I know that for a fact. But the way we should make records and stuff like that? How they compare is irrelevant to me because we just make records the way we hear them. The best thing about this record as far as I'm concerned, is that when we came back to the songs, they sounded very fresh and very relevant. We were afraid that if we left them for years and years, they might start getting dated, so we got back to them as quick as we could," said Lars (ibid: 52).

The cover was also "part II" of *Load*. With *Reload* they wanted to keep the same artist, Andres Serrano, to keep the same kind of feel to both of them. So instead of sperm and blood, this time it's blood and urine. And this is significant because in many ways *Reload* is a more blood-and-piss album than a blood-and-cum one.

Fuel

One of the strongest Metallica album openers ever, an apocalyptic biker anthem that shows some touches of Blue Öyster Cult's "Transmaniacon MC" as well as San Diego rock classicists Rocket From the Crypt, a band that James Hetfield was a big fan of in the mid-Nineties. It's about the joy of driving fast: "Gimme Fuel, Gimme Fire, Gimme that which I desire." It has no great deep meanings ("Nitro junkie" refers to the practice of injecting NO_2 [nitrous dioxide] into the fuel mix to give the engine a short-lived burst of power, pushing the vehicle beyond its normal capabilities): it's a too-fast-to-live-too-young-to-die slice of life in the rock 'n' roll fast lane, and as such became a big favourite with Playstation gamers – *Hot Wheels Turbo* and *Test Drive: Off-Road, Wide Open* both

positive, with a lot of bile being vented by fans through the still-new medium of the internet, on fan websites and in chatrooms and message boards. Lars: "I am a little miffed at the fact that here were so many people that looked at the pictures of *Load* and did not give the music a chance. Did it really make a difference in my life? Not really, but I'm surprised at that narrow-mindedness, that's all. I'm not hurt by it 'cos the record's sold as many copies as I thought it would, and the state of Metallica internally is stronger than at any point after the 'black album', so none of these things really matter that much to me. I am surprised at people's surprise over some of the things that happened to us over the last couple of years, because I thought we always wore all those potential changes and that stuff on our sleeves. Us going away for five years – what the fuck did they expect?" (*Metal Hammer*, December 97: 51).

Ulrich himself was not above winding up the fans,

included the track. NHL ice hockey team the Philadelphia Flyers used the song as their anthem before every home match for a couple of seasons, and it became a favourite track with TV news film editors to accompany footage of buildings exploding, high-speed car crashes or high-performance fighter jets.

The Memory Remains

Inspired by Billy Wilder's bleak 1950s melodrama *Sunset Boulevard*, a film about an ageing movie diva from the silent era fading away in modern-day LA, convinced that she is still a big star. "The Memory Remains" is evocative of the image of a haggard Gloria Swanson trying to shut time out of her empty mansion, all the mirrors covered over, going progressively mad: "Fortune, fame/Mirror vain/Gone insane".

Whether the addition of Marianne Faithfull, these days an all-purpose icon-for-hire, to add her throaty 60-cigarettes-a-day drunken-sailor backing vocals was one of their best ideas ever, is debatable. "We talked about instead of two of the vocal bridges being lyrics, they would just be a vocal melody that would be hummed or sung," said Lars. "And then the idea came up that the vocal melody would maybe be sung by a female instead of James. We sat down and thought about who would have a characteristic voice, with a lot of depth, but also a voice that sounded weathered and vulnerable – that list was incredibly short, it only had Marianne Faithfull's name on it." (*Metal Hammer*, December 97: 54).

The snatch of dialogue at the end over the fade-out "Say yes. At least say hello" is from the film *The Misfits*, lines spoken by Marilyn Monroe in the last film

she made before her premature death. It was apparently Marianne Faithfull's idea to include this as a sort of homage to her favourite film. According to Lars: "It's the first time a woman's sung on a Metallica album...except for Kirk." (1:102).

Devil's Dance

An ultra-heavy sludgy, almost Sabbath-like track, steeped in leaden blues riffs played with sledgehammers. Like "Sad But True" it looks at the dual nature of man, good and evil, in and out of balance, though in a more light-hearted way. The devil in the song puts temptation in man's way, but he doesn't really have to work too hard: "Yeah, I feel you too/Feel, those things you do."

The Unforgiven II

The sequel to the song from the "black" album maintains the "country" influence with the twangy guitar early on, before building to an almost Crazy Horse-inspired guitar duel at the end. "It's continuing the story," said Ulrich. "We sat down to write a piece of music and thought, Hmm, that kinda has the same flavour as 'The Unforgiven' – let's do something we've never done before, let's continue a story and see what that does for the creative vibe. That's one of the first songs we did for the *Load* sessions and actually the only song that was left off on purpose and put on *Reload*, because we really felt it would be good to have a space between the two versions… it really is just taking a story you'd started that you maybe didn't feel that you had finished and see what can be done creatively to take it somewhere else." (ibid).

It's one of the many examples of James crooning, singing ballads that would have been unthinkable before … *Justice* – though as Jason Newsted cattily remarked, all these songs had to be in the key of E to suit his limited vocal range. Overall, the song's country blues feel is reminiscent of The Rolling Stones circa *Exile On Main Street*, with its slightly washed-out, dishevelled sound.

Better than You

One of the stronger hard rock outings on *Reload* that gave the lie to any accusations that Metallica had either blanded out or turned their collective backs on hard rock. Lyrically, it's James celebrating the constant striving to be top dog that keeps you vital: "Lock horns, I push and I strive/ Somehow I feel more alive." The vocal interplay with Jason on the chorus gives it a slight death metal feel.

Slither

Another song that sounds like a homage to AC/DC, another mega-heavy retro blues riff and acidic vocals. Like many of the songs on both *Load* and *Reload* there seems to be a conscious attempt to recreate hard rock from the period before Metallica's beloved NWOBHM: the precedents here are bands like Black Oak Arkansas, .38 Special and Derringer, who were already washed-up when Metallica were barely in adolescence. The theme is about going looking for temptation: "So don't go looking for snakes you might find them/Don't send your eyes to the sun you might blind them". Snakes could represent the temptation of the serpent in Eden; as a venomous animal, the snake could also represent drugs, a world that's devoid of heroes. For a song that would make a great stadium stompalong, this is another from this era that the band have never actually played live.

Carpe Diem Baby

Apparently, James has a tattoo on his arm of some playing cards fanned out, with flames shooting up, which reads "Carpe Diem Baby". Whether this is symbolic of his attitude to life after the accident that left him with serious burns – the cards represent the hand that life deals you; "carpe diem", from the Latin "seize the day" – is anybody's guess.

"Carpe Diem Baby" is another good solid riff-heavy Metallica song about living for the here and now: "So wash your face away with dirt/It don't feel good until it hurts." According to James: "The lyrics are a lot darker, if we can get any darker! There's songs about being down and out and not accepting pity. Nothing goes your way all the time and that's just life, my friend. People don't take responsibility for themselves and that's always been a major theme of mine." (1:102).

Bad Seed

This song was originally named "Bad Seed (Bastard)" and was previewed when they jammed it at the beginning of the set caught on their video *Cunning Stunts*. It's yet another old school Metallica rocker loaded with biblical imagery (the title comes from the parable of the farmer sorting out the good from the bad seed, the wheat from the chaff in *Matthew* 13:24–30): "Off the veil/Stand revealed/Bring it on/Break the Seal" encapsulates Genesis to Revelations in a few lines. "Off the veil" refers to Adam hiding his nakedness from God "And he said, Who told thee that thou wast naked? Hast thou eaten of the tree, whereof I commanded thee that thou shouldest not eat?" (Genesis 3:11), while the Seal is the seventh one broken by the angel that heralds the end of the world. Like the Bible itself, it's vague and open to a lot of different interpretations.

*A shorn Kirk kicks out the **Load** jams.*

Where The Wild Things Are

With its title taken from Maurice Sendak's celebrated children's book, the song is about childhood and children and the possibilities they contain for both good or ill. It's also about disillusion, with striking imagery of war and violence contained in the games. Lyrically it is probably one of the best songs James has ever written. Lines like "Hand puppets storm the beach/Fire trucks trapped out of reach/" are simply inspired. James's first child, Cali Tee, was not born until 1998, at least two years after the song was written, but the tone of the song is like a father singing to a child, though the riffs are more suited to a drive-by than a lullaby.

Prince Charming

Primal angry Metallica with James writing in character as the personification of all that is evil: "I'm the nothing face that plants the bomb/And strolls away". Hetfield's vocals and Kirk's eerie psychedelic wah-wah guitar lend a really dark edge to this track.

Low Man's Lyric

Like "Mama Said" on *Load*, this was the most problematic cut on *Reload* because of its supposed folk influences. But stripping away the hurdy gurdy and the strings leaves an otherwise fairly conventional Metallica ballad."It has a lot in common with 'Mama Said' for specific reasons,' said Lars. "Me and James were really sick of writing these neat little rock ballads... So 'Mama Said' got developed and pushed in the direction of country influences. 'Low Man's Lyric', which had a working title of 'My Eyes' for many years, was sort of this rock ballad that didn't have any character or anything, so the idea came up to project in the direction of Irish folk music. James had been listening to quite a bit of Irish folk music and, through Jim Martin, had been introduced to some of these instruments. There's a well-known band called The Chieftains that were quite inspirational, and we kind of pushed the song in that direction to give it some character, just like we did with 'Mama Said'"" (ibid). It's a song from the point of view of a homeless man, though

as in "Prince Charming", he's a more universal outcast: "So low the sky is all I see/All I want from you is forgive me." It's like a throwback to the more adolescent lyrics from *Kill 'Em All* and jars with the more mature writing on *Load*, *Reload* and *Metallica*.

Attitude

Another piece of vintage hard rock, as if to compensate fans for the previous track, "Attitude" talks as tough as it sounds and while not exactly one of the stand-out tracks on *Reload* it proves that despite their professed fondness for jazz, folk and country, the influence of classic Judas Priest and Iron Maiden never really left them. Dominated by ferocious dual-lead guitars and full-throttle, bluesy energy, Hetfield sings, "Just let me kill you for a while/ Just let me kill you for a smile." Sensitive soul.

Fixxxer

The epic endpiece of the album, a sort of companion to "The Outlaw Torn" on *Load*, so despite Lars' protestations that this would be a more 'one-dimensional' album, it mirrors the structure of *Load* almost exactly. It appears to be about religion, about the psychological abuse of children, using the metaphor of a voodoo doll stuck with pins ("One for each of us and our sins") that sucks the joy out of life. But while the younger Hetfield would merely batter us with his rage, the more mature Hetfield goes beyond the anger, looking for healing: "Tell me/Can you heal what father's done?" Beginning with "treated" guitars, chopped up in the mix, fed through FX pedals, it settles into a more conventional, crunching Metallica slow groove and ends on an affirmative chord rather than fading out. A satisfying end to a less than satisfying album.

James gets medieval on the crowd's ass.

8

St Anger Interview

When Metallica reappeared touting a new album called *St Anger* in June of 2003, the fanbase rejoiced at the band's return. What's more, the music re-affirmed that Metallica's heart was firmly back into playing the fast, aggressive and progressive style that had provided them with their early victories. However, what many fans didn't realize was just how close to the brink Metallica had been during the six-year gap between 1997's *Reload* and the new record.

A cycle of four record in four years ('96's *Load*, '97's *Reload*, '98's cover's album *Garage Days* and '99's live *S&M*) had taken an exhausting toll on the band. Pushed into becoming as much a part of the music industry machine as any high-selling diva or pop starlet, Metallica started to break from within. First they were unfairly labelled as "The Man" when free music internet site Napster were targeted by the band (and their highly paid lawyers) for copyright infringement, with Lars in particular being singled out as a rich rock star "bad guy". Then in January '01 came the news that many close to the band had known for months – Jason Newsted was quitting. No one had ever quit Metallica before, and the band were shocked to their roots by Jason's accusations that they had lost their way and become the very thing that Metallica had been a reaction against.

Initially the recovery period went well for Metallica, as the band ploughed ahead with new material with producer Bob Rock, in the Presidio rehearsal studios in San Francisco. Then, some three weeks in, James Hetfield let it be known that he was entering rehab in order to find the peace of mind he felt his life lacked. James would later say that rehab was "college for his soul". However, back in Metallicaland, the weeks waiting for James's return turned into months. After nearly six months of no contact, Lars and Kirk believed that Metallica was all but over.

Then, following Kirk Hammett's 39th birthday party in late '01, where a refreshed James Hetfield made a surprise appearance, the band began to function once more. Now aided by digital technology, Metallica wrapped themselves in a new-found sense of creative freedom, and turned their backs on their self-imposed rules. James invited everyone to help out on the lyrics so that the whole band would understand where he was coming from, while Lars and Kirk both agreed to lay their music open to (constructive) criticism. The openness worked and *St Anger* was the monstrous result. The musical equivalent of a WWE rumble, *St Anger* takes its strength from the personal trials of its musical protagonists and revels in its lengthy, bellowing arrangements, which are fuelled by an almost punk/metal-like attitude reminiscent of early Metallica heroes The Misfits and Discharge.

After recording, during which producer Bob Rock handled all bass parts, the band then held a brief set of auditions to find their new member, settling for Ozzy Osbourne's four-stringer and former Suicidal Tendencies man Rob Trujillo, a surfing buddy of Kirk's. Metallica Mk III was ready to rumble...

New Kid on the Block: Rob Trujillo.

This interview took place in mid-April 2003 when the band were gearing up to unleash their first new music in six years upon an unsuspecting public.

James
The riffs are very aggressive and in your face, it is a definite step away from that highly polished sound you worked hard to achieve on the *Load* albums, isn't it?

"Oh yeah, it's aggressive alright. I don't know whether we achieved anything by contriving to step away from any previous sound, because the music that we wrote for *St Anger* is just an extension of where we are at as people. Music doesn't tell us how to be, we create the music. I think Metallica could easily have gone on to make *Unload* or *Superload* or whatever the next *Load* would've been, had our lives stayed the same as they were."

Looking back at the *Load/Reload* days, there was a very definite focus on the image of Metallica, while with *St Anger* it seems that there is very much less focus on your image. That surely must be a conscious effort to depart from before?

"*Load* was definitely a time where Lars and Kirk were stepping up and saying 'Let's try something new'. They were passionate about art and photography and so we went with it. Sure, Jason [Newsted] and I were, er, less than enthusiastic about that approach shall we say, heh, heh, but for the sake of having a band feel we went with it. Looking back it was fun, I can laugh about it now 'cause it's part of history and it's behind us. OK, so we went down a dead end but we turned ourselves around again."

There's been this wild rumour that song lyrics were worked on by all the various members this time, can that possibly be true?

"Ha! Yes it's true, everyone worked on each song together. I'm in every one, Lars came up with the basis for a few ideas, and there are major lines that came from Kirk and Bob [Rock] too.

"For me, this sharing of the lyrical workload was a

crucial step in the development of Metallica, 'cause it really helped me out. In the past I've felt like I'm the one up there shedding tears for 'Bleeding Me' while the rest of the guys are there yawning, doing what they do, 'cause they just don't feel it like I do. This time everyone feels these words deeply, because they've all touched on one subject from different angles.

"We've all had different upbringings, different fears about things and different passions too, and they all kinda show up in these shared words, I think."

So let's fast forward a few months. You made a decision to return and you collectively made a decision to write and record a new Metallica record with Bob Rock filling in on bass duties. Why did you not look for a new member at that point, someone who could help with the writing?

"Bob has walked our journey since the 'black album'. He knew what we needed, what we wanted and what we were after when we said that we wanted to write all together for the first time. He was spearheading that breakthrough. I think the three of us – Lars, Kirk and me – all felt that replacing Jason straight away would've been a mistake. When your girlfriend dumps you, you can either go straight out and replace her with another, or you can choose to look inwardly and ask why it was she left, and to what part of that did your actions make a difference. Getting over all of that stuff was paramount, and Bob bought us valuable healing time by being able to write and play the bass how we would've wanted anyone else to do it at that time."

Metallica in 2003 seems like a serene place to be – are you surprised therefore at how pissed off *St Anger* actually came out sounding, then?

"We've heard the idea that now that Metallica have managed to become comfortable with each other we must be unconsciously reacting to it, heh, heh.

"*St Anger* helps us express anger in a healthy, non-violent way. It might sound cornball now but let me tell you, in our heads at that time we wrote it, we got really way out there.

"There were still uncomfortable times in the studio where I was stuck for a melody or how to get a line, and no one will meet your gaze, but what can I say? We're still getting to re-know each other again. We all have our moments but unlike before we're not deliberately pushing at each other's weak points, we're helping each other through.

"Within this band we've each addressed our own defects of character and we've been able to point them in the same direction for the first time. You can hear that energy flowing through the record for sure... "

Kirk

***St Anger* is your first record in some six years. What's your take on the journey you've been through and where you are at right now?**

"If we had followed the 'black album' with a record like this then it would have been a half-hearted attempt at something we knew we'd already done to death. That's why we did stuff like *Load* and *S&M* and it felt good to do that.

"With this record we were following our instincts and listening to our gut reactions, and playing music which we're comfortable with.

"I gotta admit, I never want to let go of a new album. You lose a little intimacy with the music, but I guess it's what we're here to do. I always want to keep a hold as long as possible, just sit there with it and love it. It's a real selfish thing that I have whenever we work on a new record, anytime we release one it feels like I'm letting go of control. You strive to accomplish certain goals creatively and when you've hit that goal you can't help but think that you've done a great thing. It's like having a kid, you don't see the flaws or imperfections because you love them so much."

Does it feel good to be able to play music like this and have people react in such a positive way?

"I have to tell you that there is a very deep acknowledgement from within ourselves and to each other that we can kick fucking ass to show we can maintain passion, integrity, energy and commitment, and dedication and loyalty to this band – it's a beautiful thing."

James's time away from the band must have been difficult to live with, particularly after Jason Newsted's departure. Did you ever doubt your resolve during those dark times?

"Me being the person I am, I had to brace myself for the worst. I had to find out whether I could exist without Metallica. Could I have a life without Metallica? Were there enough things in my life worth pursuing? Thankfully I found out that I did have a life after a bit of soul searching. That time I spent thinking lent me a certain strength to find the patience to wait for James. It gave me a lot of hope that we could get it back on track. Slowly but surely we came back from the brink, having meetings, reconnecting with James on a personal and emotional level to see where his head was at, before we even began to start talking music or the business of Metallica."

Lars
Wasn't it a little weird to find yourselves walking into a studio to make a new record after six years away from Load?

"I wouldn't say weird, I'd say exciting. After Jason left [January 2001] me, James and Kirk spent a few months dealing with that, and then we moved into these old army barracks called Presidio before HQ was ready, to write new material. We called up Bob Rock and we were ready to go.

"The spirit at that time was a loose non-sterile, anti-studio, pro-creative mood. It was really exciting because we felt that everything we had tried to convince ourselves was right in order to make those four records in four years was being turned on its head. Kirk, James and Bob Rock sat down in a circle on the Presidio floor, and started working on music almost immediately, and for a short while it looked like we were gonna follow through. Then James came to us and said he was going away for five weeks. Then five weeks turned into two months then into three and so on...

"It was bizarre working like that in Presidio because that was the way that Jason had said Metallica should have been working for years."

Do you think St Anger is the sound of a Metallica that didn't know if it was ever going to get a chance to be a band again?

"One thing I've learned over the last year is that there seems to be this perception that if you make a very aggressive album full of angry pissed-off energy, then you have to be angry pissed-off people to do it, and I think we bought into that for many, many years too, so we learnt to tap into only the negative things in life, particularly between me and James. Our negativity would fuel our creativity, or so it seemed.

"Even our manager commented on the paradox we were facing when James returned a better man, about how were we gonna make a great pissed-off Metallica record when we were all getting along so politely. So I think we proved to ourselves and the rest of the world that you can make a pissed-off piece of work without the self-hate.

"For many of the previous records I'd wake up and mentally put on the armour to go down to the studio, with the mindset that if I could win seven of the ten arguments that the day would bring, then it had been a good day's work. And now we've made a record where we needed none of that."

Do you actually care what anyone thinks about Metallica now that you've been through all this and still come up with the goods?

"Yeah, 'course I do. The old chest-beating, I-couldn't-give-a-fuck thing in interviews is one of the easiest things to throw out, and it always looks good but you can still care what people think without it affecting what you are doing. I think there is a tendency for people to correlate those two as one thing."

But it's hardly likely that St Anger is going to match the 26 million copies sold by the "black album", is it?

"I'd be happy if something like St Anger made it to two million copies! I always try to find the good in any situation these days, so I look at it as, 'Hey, I'm glad that we are one of only ten bands that have ever had a

St Anger Interview

record that big.' *St Anger* is not going to sell anywhere near that.

"We haven't even picked the singles yet because we're just not tuned to that yet. I knew when we wrote 'Enter Sandman', I swear I knew it would be the opener on the next album, but right now there's no way I can tell you what the singles are gonna be. In fact I don't really care what they are, because it means so little to how we actually wrote the record. We'll leave any edits up to Bob Rock to do because I was the one who edited all these songs together, and I don't wanna be the one editing them apart."

And how would they say you've changed, after all you're the doting dad of two now?

"I think fatherhood has changed me profoundly. I am far more aware of my own mortality now than I ever have been before. I have become very aware of this thing people call death. When you're 25 you have a very different perspective, you think you're invulnerable, but as a father I now start seeing things in timelines and I'm a little more vulnerable too.

"Band-wise I've also learned not to spend all my energy trying to convert someone else's point of view into my own, but to spend that same energy trying to see their point of view, which can be very helpful when you're in a band, I can tell you.

"Of course it's great to read early reviews talking up the new record because we are so proud of everything we've achieved in the last two years, and it's nice that people care and that it's positive, but at the same time I really do feel that Metallica do exist in our own little universe. After a 22-year run you're bound to get ups and downs, but right now we're so inward-looking because we're so connected to each other."

What's the story behind "Frantic"?

"It was actually my lyric idea. You've heard about how we all did these songs together but it was perhaps more mine. Lyrically it's about mortality – the tick-tick-tick line in there. The first line is if I could get all my wasted days back. If you knew you had 4,212 days left, but then you

could have all the days back that you spent hungover or the ones you spent in bed? How would it affect you? So it's about how you would live your life if you knew exactly how many days left that you had."

"St Anger"?

"'St Anger' is about James's struggle with anger as an emotion. I think he says somewhere 'Anger get a bad rap'. When he was growing up, anger was never an emotion that was allowed to be on show or was ever tolerated. So it's about how everyone associates anger with violence, but is there a way of unleashing anger in a positive way? Then there's the bit about the imagery with the medallion that can protect you or strangle you. It's pretty deep stuff but graphically it lends itself as a title track because of what we can do with it."

"Dirty Window"?

"This is about that judging thing where you are telling people what to do. The line is 'I see my reflection in the window, it looks different to what you see', so it's about self-perception and how you can be guilty of doing things to other people that you'll never see yourself. There's a line about drinking from the cup of denial and judging the world from my throne."

"All Within My Hands"?

"You mean the one ending with 'Kill kill kill kill KILL!' Yeah, after we put that song together we figured that we had better put that at the end 'cause nothing was gonna follow it! It's about control – controlling everything and moulding everything in your hands. Actually, I think it's more about wanting to protect everything around you so much that you embrace it so hard, that you end up strangling those close to you."

People will assume that that's about Jason...?

"Hmm. I'm not saying anything."

Index